A WORTHY FOUNDATION

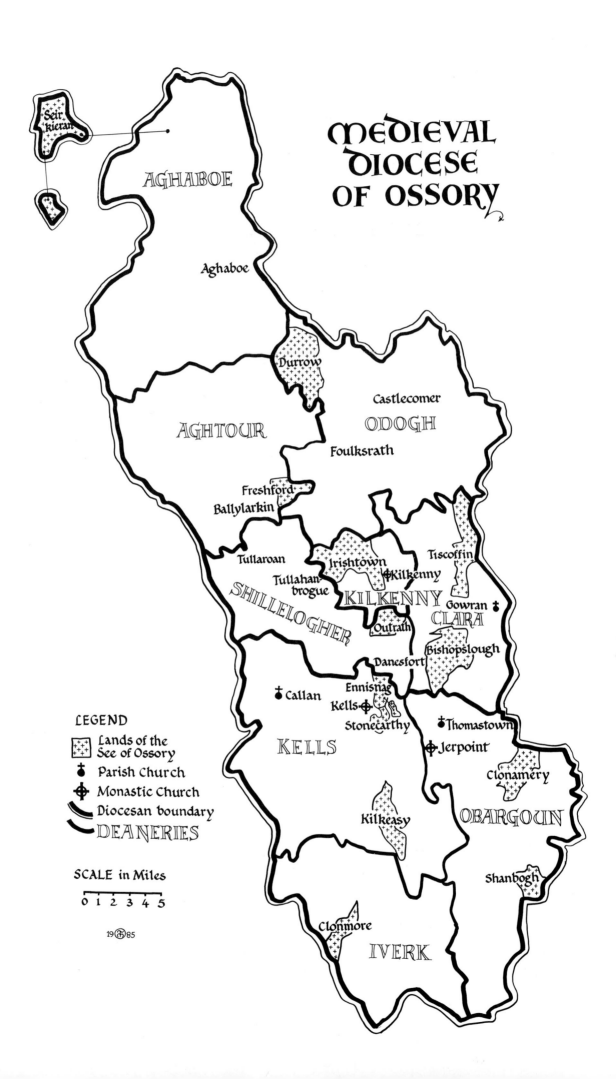

MEDIEVAL DIOCESE OF OSSORY

Seir kieran

AGHABOE

Aghaboe

Durrow

AGHTOUR

Castlecomer

ODOGH

Foulksrath

Freshford
Ballylarkin

Tullaroan

Tullahan-
brogue

SHILLELOGHER

Irishtown

KILKENNY

Kilkenny

Tiscoffin

Gowran

CLARA

Outrath

Bishopslough

Danesfort

Ennisnag

Callan

Kells

Stonecarthy

Thomastown

Jerpoint

KELLS

Clonamery

OBARGOUN

Kilkeasy

Shanbogh

Clonmore

IVERK

LEGEND

Lands of the See of Ossory

✝ Parish Church

✠ Monastic Church

Diocesan boundary

DEANERIES

SCALE in Miles

0 1 2 3 4 5

19 85

A Worthy Foundation

THE CATHEDRAL CHURCH OF
ST CANICE
KILKENNY
1285-1985

Essays by

SIUBAN BARRY
JOHN BRADLEY
ADRIAN EMPEY

Edited by Adrian Empey

THE DOLMEN PRESS

A Worthy Foundation is set in Andover type by Photo-Set Limited, Dublin
and printed in the Republic of Ireland by O'Brien Promotions Ltd. for the publishers.

The Dolmen Press Limited
Mountrath, Portlaoise, Ireland.

Designed by Liam Miller; page assembly by Photo-Set.

First published 1985.

British Library Cataloguing in Publication Data.
Barry, Siuban
A worthy foundation: the cathedral church of
St. Canice, Kilkenny 1285-1985.
1. St. Canice's Cathedral—Kilkenny
2. Cathedrals—Ireland—Kilkenny (Kilkenny)
3. Church architecture—Ireland—Kilkenny (Kilkenny)
I. Title   II. Bradley, John   III. Empey, Adrian
726'.6'094189   NA5491.K5

ISBN 0-85105-435-8 Pbk

Contents

The cover design is a reproduction of the line engraving of St Canice's in *The Antiquities of Ireland* by Francis Grose, Volume I, 1791 from an original drawing by J. G. Brien. The map of the medieval Diocese of Ossory was drawn by Timothy O'Neill FSC.

The Authors

Siuban Barry, B.A. (Mod.), M. Litt. Part-time lecturer in the National College of Art and Design, Dublin.

John Bradley, M.A. Archaeologist, and Director of the Urban Archaeology Survey, Newman House, Dublin.

Adrian Empey, M.A. Ph.D. Rector of Clane Union, and canon of St Patrick's Cathedral, Dublin.

Foreword

The passage of seven centuries and the tide of history have impressed themselves deeply on the architectural record of St Canice's Cathedral since its foundation in the early thirteenth century. Bishops have come and gone, noblemen and craftsmen have worshipped in its precincts and been remembered in its monuments. Its continued existence has been made possible only by the continuing devotion of successive generations of clergy and people who could not allow this graceful house of God to fall into decay.

We have now reached the 700th anniversary of the cathedral's life and are very grateful to the contributors for making possible this publication in celebration of a great milestone in the cathedral's on-going history.

I would particularly like to thank Dr Adrian Empey for undertaking the painstaking task of preparing the book for publication.

I hope and pray, as I am sure our readers will also wish to do, that St Canice's Cathedral will carry into the future both her continuity with the past and her unchanging purpose to serve the needs of people in search of God.

Brian Harvey, Dean of Ossory.

Introduction

'Kilkenny, the best vplandish towne, or, as they terme it, the proprest dry towne in Ireland ... hath thre churches ... S. Kennies churche is theyr chiefe and cathedrall church, a worthy foundation as well for gorgeous buildinges as for notable liuyngs'. Thus did Richard Stanyhurst, Anglo-Ireland's most distinguished man of letters in the Elizabethan period, describe the towering masonry of the cathedral church of St Canice. Behind the measured Renaissance prose one may detect an element of native pride, for it was under the shadow of St Canice's — in the building which now houses the library — that Stanyhurst was introduced to classical learning under the tutorship of Peter White, master of the famous grammar school founded by Piers Butler, earl of Ormond, and his wife Margaret Fitzgerald. In moments of inattention his gaze must often have lifted from the pages of Virgil and fixed itself on the mass of the cathedral in its ever-changing moods. A worthy foundation indeed: it would be hard to find a more fitting phrase to describe a building — by European architectural standards modest enough — which somehow expresses a sense of time and place that is peculiar to itself. The elements include the dreaming spirituality of the Celtic round tower adjoining the south transept and the earthy confidence of the soaring Gothic. Here, where the grandeur of Rheims and Salisbury would be artistically misplaced, two cultures blend incongruously in architectural embrace to produce a worthy three-dimensional expression of the *genius loci*.

It is, of course, difficult to fix a terminal date for the completion of medieval cathedrals, and in this St Canice's is no exception. The broad outline is, however, reasonably clear. Building evidently commenced in the episcopate of Hugh de Rous, the first Norman bishop, probably soon after he acceded to the see in *c.*1202. Later tradition attributes the finishing touches to Bishop Geoffrey St Leger, who died in 1287. In fact the building programme was punctuated by a series of stops and starts, and we may doubt that work was fully completed even in the time of St Leger. Nevertheless, the view that the bulk of the work was carried out between 1202 and 1287 is sustainable on critical grounds by the architectural record. Thus the choice of the year 1985 for the celebration of the seventh centenary of the completion of the cathedral is neither random nor arbitrary.

'The great and famous, most beautiful cathedral church of Saint Keney', to borrow Bishop Griffith Williams's description (1661), has naturally been the subject of a number of studies. The inspiration behind successive studies has, however, been largely antiquarian, that is to say they have been preoccupied with recording and accumulating facts about the building and its fabric. That some of this work, most notably the great history written by Graves and Prim in 1857, has been painstakingly scholarly goes without saying, but viewed from the perspective of 1985 it cannot be said to be entirely satisfactory. The story of the cathedral, after all, is more than the sum of its parts: it is substance as well as accident. There are wider historical questions which deserve examination: what forces were at work in the diocese in the thirteenth

9

century which culminated in the construction of the Gothic cathedral? What architectural influences were involved in the planning, designing, and execution of the building? How much of it was due to the work of foreign and native craftsmen? What social influences were at work in the growing demand for sepulchral monuments, particularly in the later middle ages? Thus the cathedral is more than a mass of inorganic material arranged in an artistic manner. It records with the fidelity of a seismograph changes both in the church and in society at large. It is this interplay of social and artistic form which constitutes the essential ingredient of these living stones.

In pursuing such questions we have not lost sight of more immediate concerns. Chief among these is the intention to provide a comprehensive description and assessment of the architecture and medieval monuments. Strangely enough, this much-admired building has not been extensively researched since the publication of the monumental history by Graves and Prim, although it is in this respect more than any other that their book is lacking by modern standards. Siuban Barry has undertaken the task of bridging the gap, giving at the same time a useful survey of the various restorations which the cathedral has undergone in the passage of seven centuries. John Bradley, on the other hand, draws our attention downwards to the largest and most complete collection of medieval burial monuments in Ireland, including the finest examples of tomb sculpture to be found in this island. What is equally striking is the breadth of the social spectrum represented by these monuments — churchmen, merchants, nobility, gentry, fighting-men, members of the professional classes — the relative magnificence of which perpetuates in death the social barriers created by the living. Here we have a tapestry of almost Chaucerian richness. Not surprisingly, so many 'goodly marble monuments and especially the stately and costly monument of the house of Ormonde of most rare and excellent work' have excited the admiration of more than Bishop Williams since the seventeenth century, but until now no comprehensive listing has been made.

Just as the tombs reflect the social status of those commemorated, so too the cathedral itself is a *monumentum aere perennius* intended from the outset to proclaim the power and prestige of a new type of bishop who was not merely a shepherd of the sheep, but a diocesan administrator, a feudal lord, and — as often as not — a holder of high office in the service of the crown. In my study of the diocese of Ossory I have attempted to relate the construction of the cathedral not only to this new perception of the office of bishop introduced into Ireland by the Normans, but also to the development of the episcopal and diocesan administration which made such an enterprise possible in the first place.

Because the cathedral is a work of art it deserves to be studied afresh. History is not just the accretion of more knowledge about the past: it is a dialogue between the generations. This *Festschrift* is a contribution to that on-going dialogue from the perspective of 1985. For this reason we have consciously eschewed writing another chronological 'history'. In the process we hope we have produced not just a useful though little used reference work, but something that can be read with interest and pleasure by all who have come to, seen, and been conquered by the church of St Canice.

Introduction

ACKNOWLEDGEMENTS

This enterprise could not have been undertaken without the enthusiasm of the contributors, the generosity of the sponsors, and the encouragement of individuals. In Mr Bradley and Miss Barry I discovered everything an editor could unreasonably hope for: unquestioning co-operation, stoic patience, and a readiness to meet arbitrarily-imposed deadlines. Those who are versed in the art of calligraphy will recognise the hand of Brother Timothy O'Neill, who devoted his skill in the service of St Canice in the production of the map of Ossory from my rough-hewn original. This reservoir of voluntary talent would, however, have remained untapped were it not for the generosity of Mr George Sherwood, Mr Thomas Crotty, Mr Peter Smithwick, Mr Thomas Nicholson, the members of the select vestry of the Fertagh parish, and the members of Kilkenny County Council who provided the necessary financial support to set the wheels of publication in motion. Without their practical assistance, nothing would have come of this venture.

I would like to pay tribute to the technical skill of the printers, and to the publisher, Mr Liam Miller, who somehow transformed the amorphous bundle of papers, drawings, and photographs into this most professional production. His prompt suggestions resolved problems which caused me hours of fruitless agonising; to him I owe both the title and the cover design.

The achievement of bringing together all these necessary talents must be attributed to the 'spirit of counsel and ghostly strength', which took the form variously of the Rev. Cecil Weekes, rector of Carlow, to whom I owe a debt of gratitude, the Right Rev. N.V. Willoughby, bishop of Cashel and Ossory, who has been most helpful, and my wife, June, who refused to hear my ofttimes sub-literary expressions of defeat. Without their *active* encouragement I should never have brought this to a successful conclusion.

Lastly, I wish the thank the Very Rev. Brian Harvey, dean of Ossory, for his support, and the Most Rev. G.O. Simms for his assistance in proof-reading and launching this book.

Adrian Empey
St Michael's Vicarage, Sallins.

The Anglo-Norman Diocese of Ossory

ADRIAN EMPEY

A cathedral is distinguished from other churches in a diocese only in that it possesses the oldest insignia of the bishop's authority, the *cathedra* or bishop's seat. In a wider sense, however, the scale and grandeur of the building in relation to other ecclesiastical structures of the same period may be regarded as an architectural statement about the nature of episcopacy and its relationship to society in general. That the cathedral church of St Canice happens to be the most imposing thirteenth century edifice in the diocese of Ossory, in spite of the best efforts of the Cistercians and Augustinians not to let the case go by default, is no historical accident. Put simply, we may say that no pre-Norman bishop could have undertaken an architectural project on this scale, not only because he lacked the diocesan resources, but because episcopacy counted for much less. The great reforming councils certainly dreamed of creating a diocesan system, but in assigning specific territories to episcopal oversight they overlooked the more essential task of creating the necessary diocesan structures without which the bishop could be little more than a figurehead. The real driving force in the pre-Norman church was channelled through the new continental orders, the Cistercians and the Augustinians. Jerpoint is both the symbol and the reality of this situation: it had no architectural rival in the twelfth century. On the other hand, the towering masonry of St Canice's effectively symbolizes a decisive shift in the balance of ecclesiastical power from the monastic to the secular church. It reflects the power and self-confidence of an entirely different breed of bishop. At no time in the history of the diocese did bishops wield such a combination of spiritual and temporal power. The cathedral is therefore the expression of Norman episcopacy at the zenith of its achievement. It is a visual confirmation of the bishop's new-found confidence and social rank.

Thus there is more to the cathedral than meets the eye. We are concerned with something more fundamental than a revolution in architectural style: we are talking about a revolution in episcopal style which occurred simultaneously in Ireland. In order to understand the implications of this change we must examine the basic structure of the new episcopal order.

The transition from one style of episcopacy to another is evident if we contrast Gelasius, the saintly Irish archbishop of Armagh who visited Henry II in Dublin in 1172, and William fitz John, bishop of Ossory 1302-17. Concerning the former Gerald of Wales tells us that 'wherever he went he took with him a white cow, and lived only on its milk'[1]. His Spartan bearing breathes the spirit of twelfth century monastic rigour with echoes of an age-long tradition of Celtic spirituality. In Norman eyes, of course, an archbishop was *ex officio* one of the most powerful magnates in the realm, occupying a prominent place in the counsels of the king: one thinks almost instinctively of Hubert Walter, archbishop of Canterbury, who governed England during the greater part of the reign of Richard I. Henry's astonishment on seeing the archiepiscopal cow can only be imagined.

13

An incident of a rather different kind occurred in the town of New Leighlin (now Old Leighlin) in 1305 when William fitz John was passing through. It seems that the bishop's equipage attracted the attention not only of the awed townsmen but of the dog of one Ralph le Tannere, which attacked the attendant of one of the bishop's valets. The incident sparked off a pitched battle between the members of the equipage determined to defend one of their own, and the outraged men of Leighlin, who sought to vindicate the honour of Ralph le Tannere and his noble dog. In the ensuing fracas several of the valets were wounded: one mortally, or so it was believed; another from an arrow, while the bishop, who tried to patch up the peace, was narrowly missed by a stone aimed in his direction. No less than thirty-six townsmen, including the provost, were subsequently indicted before Edmund Butler in the assizes at Carlow, and only three of them were acquitted of the charges brought against them by the bishop. This episode reveals how far we have progressed in little more than a century — from a solitary cow to a large liveried retinue which accompanied the bishop in a display of status after the manner of the great magnates. Unlike the monkish Gelasius — whom one feels was dragged screaming from the cloister — William was immersed in the affairs of state, serving the king on occasion as chancellor and viceroy (*custos*) in the Irish administration. What distinguished him from Gelasius was not just a matter of temperament but of concepts of episcopacy which were poles apart: the spirit of the cloister was replaced by the demands of the affairs of the realm. No doubt William did not lack pastoral gifts, but in his long absences from his diocese he probably had little opportunity to exercise them. His situation called for other talents: skill in the administration of royal and ecclesiastical courts, in finance, and in diplomacy.

While the pre-Norman church under the influence of the reform movement of the twelfth century was working to establish a territorial episcopacy, there can be little doubt that the real impetus towards change came as a direct consequence of the Normanisation of the diocese. Whatever diocesan structures may have existed before this — and there is no evidence of any — were swept away by the newcomers in their impatience to replace the insular eccentricities of the Irish church with the systematic, hierarchical command-structure of the continental church, deriving ultimately from the Frankish imperial church, but refined and tested by two centuries of Norman lordship. The Irish church was to be fully integrated not only into the continental ecclesiastical system but into the framework of the Anglo-Norman state as well. It was made to measure. The changes which took place in Ossory in the early years of the thirteenth century — in diocesan organization, in the administration of episcopal manors, and in relations with the crown — were therefore part of a wider development, which incidentally provided the logistical basis for the construction of the great cathedral church of St Canice.

I

The purpose of a cathedral was to provide suitable physical conditions to permit an elaborate routine of daily worship by a body of men set apart for that purpose. The recitation of the seven canonical hours and the daily celebration of high mass were the essential ingredients of this programme of worship in the mother church of the diocese. The regulation of this worship in the almost continual absence of the bishop fell to the dean and chapter. Thus the organization of the chapter was first in the order of priority under the new ecclesiastical regime, taking precedence even over the construction of a suitable edifice. Whatever building stood on the site of the present cathedral at the beginning of the thirteenth century would have been quite inadequate for this purpose.

There can be little doubt that no chapter existed before the coming of the Normans. Outside Dublin, or at any rate the Norse sees, chapters simply did not exist. If there had been one in Ossory it would certainly have been monastic: the creation by the Normans of a secular chapter clearly suggests that nothing existed before the conquest. The fact that cathedral dignitaries during the episcopate of the last Gaelic bishop of Ossory were all Norman provides positive evidence that the organisation of the chapter was solely a Norman achievement. We may therefore assign the beginnings of cathedral organisation to the last decade of the twelfth century when the offices of dean and archdeacon were occupied by Odo and Gilbert respectively[2]. The emergence of these dignitaries strongly suggests that the see was transferred from Aghaboe to Kilkenny in the latter years of Bishop Felix's episcopate (1178-1202). As a Cistercian, Felix doubtless shared the objectives of twelfth century reform, and must have welcomed the opportunity to further them by co-operating with the newcomers.

Like many contemporary English cathedrals, the four major dignitaries consisted of the dean, precentor, chancellor, and treasurer, though in common with other Irish cathedrals the archdeacon was reckoned to be a dignitary also (ranking after the dean and before the treasurer and chancellor in a capitular instrument dated between 1245 and 1250.) The dean was president of the chapter and had cure of souls of all cathedral clergy. The precentor was responsible for music and liturgy. The chancellor was in charge of the seal of the chapter and was responsible for supervising the schools of grammar and theology (assuming these existed in Kilkenny). The treasurer looked after the cathedral's treasures, including relics and church furnishing. The archdeacon, though reckoned as a dignitary, had no important cathedral function beyond that of an ordinary prebendary since his duties naturally prevented his continual presence. Unlike monastic chapters, where members of the chapter were maintained out of the common fund, each dignitary and canon was assigned his own income: the dean, for instance, derived a personal income from burgages in St Patrick's parish; the archdeacon held some land in Kilfane. The canons lived off the income from their prebends. How long it took for the chapter to attain its final shape — consisting of five dignitaries, if we include the archdeacon, and seven prebendaries — is impossible to say, but the process was well advanced by the time Bishop Hugh died (1218), and was probably complete before the work on the building of the cathedral got into full swing as the century progressed.

Apart from the administration of the cathedral, the chief function of the chapter was to provide for the canonical election of bishops. In the early thirteenth century chapters wielded considerable independence and often 'got their man' despite pressure from royal or aristocratic lobbies. Although William Marshal, earl of Pembroke and lord of Leinster, opposed the chapter's choice of Peter Malveisin in 1219, they succeeded in the end, aided by the fact that the earl obliged them by dying in the middle of the dispute. The corporate spirit, often refined by years of battling with bishops, could be felt by the dean too. In 1388, for example, the chapter granted the dean, Michael Delafield, a set of vestments on condition that if he lost or failed to return them he would forfeit forty shillings. On occasion the dean and chapter were appointed custodians of the temporalities of the see *sede vacante* by the crown: thus Dean Adam de Trillek and the chapter of St Canice were charged at the exchequer to

15

account for the temporalities of the bishopric from the morrow of the close of Easter 1332 to 20 November following. They were allowed £20 by the treasurer and barons 'for labour and expenses in connection with the custody of the temporalities'[3], and having paid over various sums they were declared quit.

The original purpose of furnishing canons with prebends was to enable them to maintain their houses in the close, render hospitality, and spend long periods in residence in order to perform their liturgical duties. In practice, however, the canons were unable to fulfil their residential quotas, so they had to appoint *vicars* in their stead and be partially responsible for their maintenance. Although Bishop Geoffrey St Leger (1260-87) is credited with founding the college of vicars choral in Kilkenny, we may reasonably suppose that he did not introduce them but sought to regularize and better endow a body of clergy that was already in existence. It was probably Geoffrey who assigned the income from the cathedral parish towards the costs of the Common Hall. In 1450 the vicars of the Common Hall petitioned the Irish Parliament to ease the load of taxation on the Irishtown especially 'during the time the said commons [of the Irishtown] plough or sow lands in the parish of St Canice ... whereby the divine service of God may be more augmented and enforced there, and the said vicars supported to perform it'[4]. They claimed that their livings and goods had been so wasted by Irish enemies they were not able 'to continue hospitality at any time, or to sustain there the divine service'[5]. The ensuing legislation was re-enacted in a later parliament in the reign of Edward IV, with the proviso that whereas

> many of the faithful English burgesses and commons of the said Irishtown are dead and many of the Irish nation come and dwell there in their places who have refused to pay the said annual rent [six marks] to the said vicars ... to the great hurt of the said vicars and diminution of divine service in the aforesaid church. [Enacted that in the case of rent unpaid for space of two months after specified feasts] it will be lawful for the ordinary or vicar general ... to fulminate the censures of the church against every person in the Irishtown who retains the said rent ... until they make full satisfaction.[6]

In spite of the dread censures of the church, however, the denizens of the Irishtown seem never to have acquired the habit of haste in the payment of their dues to the vicars, for on 9 July 1546 the portreeve, burgesses and commons of the Irishtown, assembled in their hundred, decreed that the portreeve

> shall call before him all such collectors of the priesten mony as are in arrear to the Vicars of the Common [Hall], and shall appointe auditors to hear and see what discharge they gave for the severall monyes due by them, and if the auditors doe find them to have neglected to collecte the same, that they shall be committed [to the town jail] by the Portrive, and there to remayn untill they putte in sufficiente securitye to save harmelesse the corporacion from enny losse or harme that might ensue by means of the Vicars of the Hall.[7]

While the changes wrought by the Normans at the top of the diocesan pyramid are plain enough, we must not overlook the quiet revolution which was taking place at the base itself. The great Irish reforming councils of the twelfth century had tried — and failed — to introduce tithes, and in so doing had neglected to establish a parochial system. It remained for the Norman lords, great and small, to accomplish this task. Since the gift of the tithes of their tenants lay within the power of these lords the new parishes were fashioned out of the newly-arrived manor, as I have shown clearly in the

16

case of the cantred of Knocktopher[8]. Thus the parochial system was a direct consequence of the process of subinfeudation. The significance of this development should not escape us: the parish was the basic unit of the secular church. Without it, no secular church — and therefore no basis for episcopal authority — could be said to exist: a bishop without a parochial infrastructure could exercise no effective control over the population of his diocese. While it is true that Norman lords tended to lavish tithes on their monastic foundations, especially on the new Augustinian houses in the diocese, the bishop still exercised some control over vicars serving in parishes impropriate to monastic foundations. In the later middle ages the monastic hold on parishes became a considerable obstacle to the exercise of the bishop's pastoral oversight, but that still lay in the future. Slightly less than half of the parishes in the diocese were attached to monastic foundations.

Just as the strength of a chain is equal to its weakest link, so too the effectiveness of episcopal authority depended on the links in its command structure. The most important role in this sphere was undoubtedly that assigned to the archdeacon, who by means of his court and powers of visitation kept a close eye on the clergy and even on the population at large (in particular in matrimonial cases). Like the contemporary royal justices in eyre, the archdeacon conducted his investigations according to detailed questions set out in his *articuli,* and was empowered to impose stiff penalties on lay and clerical offenders alike. He was the *oculus episcopi,* the eye of the bishop. What the clergy called him is not recorded, or perhaps even recordable, but their resentment was given theological expression by a correspondent of John of Salisbury who reckoned that for the race of men rejoicing in the name of archdeacon there was no possibility of salvation. Something of this popular resentment may underly the presentment of a jury made before the justiciar, John Wogan, in Castlecomer on 4 December 1305:

> The twelve jurors present that ... Master Maurice le Deveneys, official of the said bishop [of Ossory], and that Master Nicholas de Donymegan [Dunnamaggan], official of the archdeacon of Ossory, hold pleas in the court of Christianity before them, which are not testamentary or matrimonial, such as pleas involving questions of good faith and defamation, as if one calls another 'meretrix' [whore].[9]

The presentment was, of course, the jury's response to a routine question about the operation of church courts, but in their reply one senses a popular irritation with the prying of ecclesiastical courts, and an unexpressed hope that the officials concerned might be hauled before a wrathful royal justice to face a stiff fine for presuming to entertain in their courts pleas which belonged of right to the king. In this case the archdeacon's official was not only the bishop's eye but his ear also. It illustrates just how meticulous was the operation of episcopal courts under the Norman bishops: no sparrow was allowed to fall without either a stiff fine or at least a dispensation.

But the presentment is interesting for other reasons. It shows that the archdeacon had not only his own official (or deputy), but a rival in the form of the bishop's official. In the early thirteenth century we sometimes find the dean acting as the bishop's official, but clearly the two offices were quite distinct by the end of the thirteenth century. The whole structure of episcopal government had become more sophisticated and diversified.

Just as the sheriff of the county was assisted by a serjeant attached to each cantred, so too the bishop had a rural dean in every deanery. The taxation of 1320 notes the existence of some nine deaneries: Kells, Obargon, Iverk, Kilkenny, Clara, Shillelogher,

Aghtour, Odogh, and Aghaboe. As in England, where the deanery tended to follow the boundaries of the hundred or wapentake, so in Ireland they tended to correspond to the cantred, or to combinations of the cantred. The rural dean had the supervision of the clergy within his deanery, together with their churches and other buildings. Another of his functions was to communicate the bishop's mandates to the clergy at the monthly ruridecanal chapters: thus Bishop Ledrede concluded his synodal decrees of *c.*1320 with an injunction to his deans to provide the clergy with transcripts within a specified period.

The effect of all these administrative measures was to impose a firm episcopal discipline both on the parochial clergy and on the population at large. Episcopal power and prestige were at their zenith, but neither of these things sufficed to build a cathedral. That is very much a question of resources. We must therefore take a closer look at the resources of the bishopric.

II

If the Norman bishops found that the pastoral administration of the diocese left much to be desired, they were fortunate in that they were heirs to an appreciable amount of land. The territorial core consisted of ancient termon lands: Seirkieran, Aghaboe, Freshford, Tullaherin, and, of course, Kilkenny-Irishtown. Before the conquest these were presumably controlled by erenaghs, who as men with an hereditary interest may not have been too intendant to the bishop. Such a system could hardly have been tolerated by a new breed of book-balancing bishops intent on squeezing every penny from every conceivable right and jurisdiction. The danger from encroachment by Norman lay lords like Theobald Walter — who was excommunicated by Bishop Felix for interfering with episcopal lands — may have been the product of genuine misunderstanding: Gaelic bishops almost certainly had no title deeds to their lands, while erenaghs must have been difficult to distinguish from other laymen.

We may suppose that the new bishops threw themselves as energetically into the task of securing and exploiting their lands as they did into the business of diocesan reorganization. The agreement made between Hugh le Rous, the first Norman bishop, and William Marshal, whereby the former exchanged his lands around Aghaboe for others more convenient, was almost certainly part of a comprehensive programme of rationalization in the opening decade of the thirteenth century. In due course these territories surface in our records in the form of the manors of Durrow, Freshford (*alias* Uppercourt), Kilkenny (*alias* Oldcourt), Bishopslogh (with Tullaherin and Ballynaboley), Tiscoffin, Outrath, Ennisnag, Kilkeasy, Clonamery, and Clonmore. The manor of Seirkieran, though physically situated in the medieval county of Tipperary, would probably have been administered as an outlying portion of County Kilkenny. Besides these, the manors of Stonecarthy and Shanbogh were held of the bishop by hereditary lay tenants and therefore do not usually appear in the inventories. Altogether these lands incorporated about 47,000 statute acres. By comparison, the territorial resources of the Cistercian houses of Jerpoint and Duiske were insignificant.

While a lordship of this size would not have warranted the bishop a place among the great magnates, it certainly placed him comfortably in the ranks of the powerful honorial barons and lesser tenants-in-chief. Moreover, the bishops exploited their resources to a much greater degree than lay lords with lordships of a comparable size.

18

In the case of a secular lordship the great proportion of the land would be controlled by their knights and free tenants, whereas all but two of the manors of the see of Ossory were reserved in demesne in the thirteenth century. Furthermore, a high proportion of these possessed towns: Irishtown, Freshford, Durrow, and probably others in Tiscoffin, Clonmore, and Bishopslogh[10]. The consequence of this policy of careful stewardship was that the temporalities of the see of Ossory yielded a much larger revenue than a secular lordship of a comparable size. At the height of their prosperity in the second half of the thirteenth century they yielded an annual revenue of about £300 a year, which probably represents about half of the annual revenue of the Butler lordship (a mere 750,000 acres) in the same period[11].

While we know little about the detail of the bishop's seignorial organisation, we have no reason to suppose that it differed from that of the surrounding lordships. Like the lay lords, the administration of his manors was under the direction of his seneschal, whose chief function was to oversee an army of bailiffs, constables, and receivers responsible for the collection of rents and revenues and for the day to day running of demesnes, mills, manor courts, town courts, markets, fairs, and so forth. Like the archdeacon and official, he attracted adverse criticism from the jury at Castlecomer in 1305, which complained that 'William de Merton, chaplain, seneschal of the bishop of Ossory, when anyone is amerced before him in the court of his lord, amerces him at will without any taxation made'[12]. The court in which the seneschal presided was a seignorial court. As such, it was quite distinct from the ecclesiastical courts.

Although Ossory could not compare with the archdiocese of Dublin in wealth, it was nevertheless one of the richer bishoprics — better off certainly than the archdiocese of Cashel and the diocese of Leighlin which bordered on it. The point which should not escape us is that St Canice's Cathedral was built precisely at the time when the temporalities of the see had attained the height of their prosperity. The fact that the cathedral is among the largest Gothic structures in Ireland is directly related to the resources of the bishopric. Significantly, the rather impoverished see of Leighlin was unable to rival the architectural glories of Ossory.

III

Since we are concerned with the cathedral as a symbol of Norman episcopacy, we cannot altogether ignore the bishop's wider responsibilities which extended beyond his *cure* and the administration of his estates. That the bishop should be deeply involved in affairs of state may seem strange today, but it was a natural consequence of the close ties which existed between church and state in this period. Of course relations between the two might be strained at times — the murder of Archbishop Becket for example — but apart from the occasional hiccup things ran smoothly according to an elaborate set of rules. The intricacy of this partnership is illustrated by the procedures adopted in the election of a bishop. The king acknowledged that the chapter had the exclusive right to elect, and that the pope and metropolitan must sanction it. On the other hand the church acknowledged that the bishop was a tenant of the crown in respect of his temporalities, and that the bishop had to render to Caesar the things that were Caesar's. Thus the chapter had to obtain a royal licence to proceed with the election, and obtain the royal assent after the election. While the king could not undo the election — unless the rules had not been properly adhered to — he had every right to refuse to restore the temporalities of the see to the bishop elect: not quite a veto but the next best thing. Thus — to take a random example — the king wrote to the justiciar of Ireland, the archbishop of Tuam, on 8 April 1287 indicating his assent to the election of the dean of St Canice to the bishopric of Ossory. Before restoring the temporalities the new bishop had first to do fealty to the justiciar for his lands, and his election had to be duly sanctioned by the metropolitan. While the bishop was excused making the journey to Dublin in person to swear fealty to the king, he was required to furnish the justiciar with a written assurance that the dispensation would not be used by any successor as a precedent.

The point behind this fancy diplomatic footwork was the royal insistence that while the bishop owed absolute allegiance to the pope in respect of his episcopal office, he owed an equally exclusive allegiance to the crown in respect of his lordship, the temporalities of the see of Ossory: in short, the king exercised the same feudal rights over the bishop as he did over his lay tenants-in-chief in respect of tenements held of the crown. Besides, the entire relationship between church and state hinged precisely on the relationship which existed between the king and the bishops. The bishops were no ordinary tenants-in-chief: they provided the key to the partnership of church and state, and in the absence of any civil service the co-operation of the church was essential. Small wonder that the king depended heavily on the Irish bishops to provide the necessary combination of skill and administrative experience to run the government in Dublin. We have already noted in passing the archbishop of Tuam and William fitz John, bishop of Ossory, who occupied the viceregal posts of justiciar and custos respectively, but of course there were many others, including a goodly selection of bishops from Kilkenny. The career of Geoffrey de Tourville, bishop of Ossory 1244-50, is not untypical of this type of civil servant bishop: chamberlain of the exchequer 1226; itinerant justice 1230; deputy chancellor 1232-4; treasurer 1234-50; and deputy justiciar 1245-6.

While royal favour must have played a significant part in the advancement of such men in the church, and the demands of high office have withdrawn them for long periods from their dioceses, we should not assume they were uncaring pastors for that reason. A letter from Pope Innocent IV to Geoffrey de Tourville suggests that the latter was deeply concerned by the fact that some of his clergy had wives (*uxores*), and that fathers passed on their benefices to their sons, and more besides. Geoffrey's predecessor, on the other hand, had to be sharply reproved by Pope Gregory X some ten years previously (1240) for his prolonged absence from his diocese, despite the fact that he never occupied an important position in the royal administration.

In view of the vital role played by the bishops in the scheme of royal government, it is not surprising that the king took extraordinary measures to ensure that they remained in his constitutional grasp. One way of securing their position in relation to the crown was to ensure that they held their lands directly from the king like other magnates of the realm. He treated the temporalities of the bishops as fiefs, dispatching his escheator to take them into his hand on the death of the bishop. For as long as the see was vacant — sometimes for years — the revenues of the temporalities were paid directly into the royal exchequer, and the government exercised the right to appoint clergy to all benefices in the gift of the bishop (thus by sharing out prebends the crown could ensure its influence in the chapter and consequently in the election of the next bishop). While such measures originated in Normandy and were applied generally in England, King John went one step further in Ireland by laying down that church land — called 'crossland' — situated within the great liberties was subject to royal jurisdiction even *sede plena* (i.e. when no vacancy existed). The effect of this measure was to declare out of bounds almost all church land in the diocese of Ossory to the officers of William Marshal, lord of the liberty of Leinster. No pleas arising in the crosslands were justiciable in the court of the liberty of Leinster, or subsequently in the court of the liberty of Kilkenny. The earl's writ literally expired at the Bregagh: the men of the episcopal manor of Kilkenny (later called Oldcourt), which included the borough of the Irishtown, were not subject in any way to the sheriff of the liberty of Kilkenny. The bishop's tenants in fact came under the jurisdiction of the royal sheriff of Dublin throughout the thirteenth century and the first three decades of the fourteenth. Technically, the Irishtown, together with all the remaining episcopal manors, lay in the medieval county of Dublin. Thus in 1317 both the bishop and the men of the crosslands of Ossory ('la communaute de la crosce de Ossoery')[13] protested to the king against the extortions of the sheriff of Dublin when he came to Ossory to hold his court (called the tourn).

Not surprisingly the device of attaching church land in far-away Ossory to the royal county of Dublin proved to be too cumbersome. A simpler solution, which seems to have been adopted generally in the Irish liberties around 1330, was to form the scattered crosslands of Ossory into a distinct royal county — the county of the cross of Ossory — with its own royal sheriff. Like the seneschal of the liberty of Kilkenny, the sheriff had to render account for his county at the prescribed terms in the exchequer in Dublin. Thus Henry fitz Robert Arnold, sheriff of the county of the cross of Kilkenny, rendered account for the crosslands of Kilkenny from September 1333 to January 1335. Among other things he was required to produce £2 for the arrears of his predecessor, John de Pembrok, who was probably the first sheriff of the cross of Kilkenny. William Outlaw, the celebrated son of Alice Kyteler, is cited on the sheriff's account as owing 1s. 8d. because 'he had not Master Theobald de Donnyemegan, official of Ossory, whom he mainprised'[14]. Presumably William had failed to produce the bishop's official in the county court of the cross although pledged to do so: perhaps he had had enough of Ledrede, though one would have thought he might have indulged in a little sinful pleasure in hauling his official before the court.

To sum up: the county of the cross, which consisted mainly of the lands of the see of Ossory, was a royal sanctuary surrounded on all sides by the private jurisdiction of the lord of Kilkenny. By such means the king was able to demonstrate his exclusive claim to the allegiance of the principal tenant in the crosslands, the bishop. That the bishop had no equal in his diocese owed something to the supervision of the crown, ensuring that he did not fall prey to the pervasive influence of the great magnates.

IV

Le style est l'homme, or, to paraphrase Buffon, the cathedral is the bishop. This formula, of course, applied to a greater or lesser degree in every corner of Christendom in the great age of cathedral building. In Ireland, however, the construction of cathedral churches only began with the 'episcopalisation' of the church brought about by an entirely new breed of bishop introduced by the Normans. What occurred in Ireland was foreshadowed to some extent by the Normanisation of the Anglo-Saxon church after 1066, where episcopal sees were transferred to centres of population and government (Chester, Chichester, Salisbury, and Lincoln for example), chapters reorganised, and the clergy subjected to a much tighter episcopal regime. Gone were the easy-going ways and insular eccentricities of the pre-conquest church. The

21

A Worthy Foundation

transition, rapid and doubtless painful, was marked by a spate of cathedral building, in many cases — symbolically enough — requiring the demolition of earlier buildings to make way for the new order. Such measures were applied in Ireland, the diocese of Ossory being itself a classic example: the transfer of the see to Kilkenny from the remote monastic mists of Aghaboe, the creation of the chapter, the introduction of a clerical police force in the form of the archdeacon and his deans, the demolition of the pre-Norman church and its substituion by the massive presence of the Gothic building.

But if the spirit of discipline was new to the English church, the episcopal system was not: in England the church had only to be adapted to the continental model. In Ireland, on the other hand, there was virtually no pre-conquest ecclesiastical famework on which to graft the Norman system: only monks in episcopal orders with no chapter, no archdeacons, no parishes, and nothing a Norman bishop would have regarded as architecturally fitting to serve as a cathedral. What occurred in Ireland was therefore no mere adaptation, but an ecclesiastical revolution which compressed into the work of one generation the achievements of several centuries of diocesan evolution. There were naturally limits to the ambitious programme of episcopalisation, for nowhere in Ireland, with the solitary exception of the diocese of Dublin, were there sufficient resources at the disposal of the bishop to build on the scale of Salisbury or Lincoln. Instead the Norman bishops in Ireland had to settle for something more modest, but in a way more appropriate to the situation of the Irish church. The simplicity of St Canice's captures something of that grandeur in which modesty is an essential element.

FOOTNOTES

1. Giraldus Cambrensis, *Expugnatio Hibernica*, ed. A.B. Scott and F.X. Martin (Dublin, 1978), p. 99.
2. See the confirmation and collation of the church of Killinthy by Felix, bishop of Ossory, in *Ir. mon. deeds, 1200-1600*, p. 302. This deed must have been drafted some time after 1192 when the subinfeudation of central Ossory was in progress. Besides, the priory of Kells was founded in the same year, so we may presume that the collation was made about this time or shortly afterwards.
3. Account of Master Adam de Trillek in *P.R.I. rep. D.K., 43*, pp 62-3.
4. Parliament held at Drogheda, 1450 (*Stat. Ire., Henry VI*, pp 209-11).
5. Ibid.
6. *Stat. Ire., 12-22 Edw. IV*, pp 315-17.
7. *The Corporation Book of the Irishtown of Kilkenny, 1537-1628*, ed. J. Ainsworth, in *Anal. Hib.*, no. 28 (1978), pp 16-17.
8. Empey, 'Medieval Knocktopher: a study in manorial settlement' in *Old Kilkenny Review*, ii (1983), pp 451-2.
9. *Cal. justic. rolls Ire., 1305-7*, pp 474-5.
10. Bishop Geoffrey de Tourville obtained a licence from the king to hold a weekly market and an annual fair in Tiscoffin and Clonmore (besides Irishtown, Durrow and Freshford) on 28 Oct. 1245 (*Cal. chart. rolls, 1226-57*, p. 289). Such rights were normally attached only to manors with towns. There is no contemporary evidence of a borough at Tullaherin (manor of Bishopslogh), but I have encountered a reference to burgage tenures there in an undated rental — probably early 17th century — in the episcopal archive, The Palace, Kilkenny. This suggests the remains of a deserted medieval borough.
11. Between 6 Jan. and 24 July 1287 the escheator accounted for a total of £171-15-4 of the issues of the temporalities of the see (*P.R.I. rep. D. K. 37*, p. 34), and between 1 Aug. 1289 and 6 Feb. 1290 he accounted for £177-0-5 (ibid., p. 40). Each account corresponds roughly to one accounting term (Easter and Michaelmas respectively), so together they make up the equivalent of one year's revenue. The evidence of thirteenth and fourteenth century extents of Butler manors in Limerick,

Tipperary, and Kilkenny indicates that the projected income of the lordship in the late thirteenth century must have been in the region of £600 a year.

12. Pleas before John Wogan 4 Dec. 1305 (*Cal. justic rolls Ire., 1305-17*, p. 474).
13. G.O. Sayles (ed.), *Documents on the affairs of Ireland before the king's council* (Dublin, 1979), nos 116 and 117
14. *P.R.I. rep. D.K. 44*, p. 40.

BIBLIOGRAPHICAL NOTE

The medieval church is the subject of an enormous body of literature, so I will confine myself to studies which have either a general or a particular bearing on my theme.

The Normanization of the Irish church may be profitably compared to a similar process which took place in the English church after 1066. Heinrich Böhmer's classic *Kirche und Staat in England und in der Normandie im XI. und XII. Jahrhundert* (Leipzig, 1899) is still an excellent analysis of this process. On the Norman church in Ireland see J.A. Watt, *The church and the two nations in medieval Ireland* (Cambridge, 1970) and *The church in medieval Ireland* (Dublin, 1972).

Although Ossory is well served by Canon W. Carrigan's four volume *History and antiquities of the diocese of Ossory* (Dublin, 1901), which contains a mine of information, it is seriously lacking by contemporary historiographical standards. For a good introduction to cathedral organization see K. Edwards, *The English secular cathedrals in the middle ages* (2nd ed. Manchester, 1967); also G.J. Hand, 'Medieval cathedral chapters' in *Ir. Cath. Hist. Comm. Proc.*, 1956, pp 11-14, and other articles by the same author; and K.W. Nicholls, 'Medieval Irish cathedral chapters' in *Archiv. Hib.*, xxi (1973), pp 102-11 (essential reading). For diocesan organization see A. Hamilton Thompson, 'Diocesan organization in the middle ages: archdeacons and rural deans' in *Proc. British Academy*, xxix (1943), pp 153-94; P. Andrieu-Guitrancourt, *Essai sur l'évolution du décanat rural en Angleterre d'après les conciles de xiie, xiiie, et xive siècles* (Paris, 1935). I have underlined the association of cantreds with deaneries in my 'Cantreds of the medieval county of Kilkenny' in *R.S.A.I. Jn.*, ci (1971), pp 128-34. On the formation of parishes see the classic studies by J. Otway-Ruthven, 'Parochial development in the rural deanery of Skreen' in *R.S.A.I. Jn.*, xciv (1964), pp 111-22, and K.W. Nicholls, 'Rectory, vicarage and parish in the western Irish dioceses', ibid., ci (1971), pp 53-84.

The connection between the crown and the temporalities of the church may be explored in its English context in Margaret Howell, *Regalian right in medieval England* (London, 1962), and in its wider European context in E. Lesne, 'Les origines du droit de régalé in *Nouvelle revue historique de droit français et étranger*, xlv (1921), pp 5-52.

Although Ossory, relative to other Irish sees, is rich in source material, it is too scattered to detail here. The most important source is the Liber Ruber Diocesis Ossoriensis in the episcopal archive, Kilkenny, but the thirteenth century is better represented in the fragments of the Liber Albus published by H.F. Berry in *R.I.A. Proc.*, c (1907-9), Section C, pp 115-25. The Ormond deeds constitute another valuable source, particularly those published by N.B. White, *Irish monastic and episcopal deeds, 1200-1600* (Dublin, 1936). The Pipe Rolls of the Irish exchequer provide much information about the see lands (see 37th, 38th, 43rd, 44th, 45th, and 47th *Reports of the deputy keeper of the public records in Ireland*). In addition to these one must consult a wide range of state papers: the published calendars of patent and close rolls of both England and Ireland, the charter rolls, the justiciary rolls, and the pipe rolls. Much of this material may be conveniently found in the five volumes of the *Calendar of documents relating to Ireland* (London, 1875-86). The *Calendar of entries in the papal registers relating to Great Britain and Ireland*, together with M. P. Sheehy (ed.), *Pontificia Hibernica: medieval papal chancery documents concerning Ireland* (2 vols, Dublin, 1962-5), are essential sources for any study of the papal dimension of diocesan history.

Abbreviations and short titles are adopted from T. W. Moody (ed.), *Rules for contributors to Irish Historical Studies* (2nd ed., Dublin, 1968).

The Architecture of the Cathedral

SIUBAN BARRY

It is a large Fabrick, built on an eminence with a Descent all round it. You enter the Church-yard from the Town by a Flight of Marble steps; it is planted with regular Trees, and to the west a handsome Terrace-Walk, where you have a beautiful Prospect of a very fine Country . . . in short my Lord, it is a noble Pile of *Gothic* Building[1].

I

Of the many fine buildings erected by the Anglo-Norman invaders St Canice's Cathedral, Kilkenny, is one of the few which has survived virtually intact, having escaped destruction, decay, and over-zealous restoration, that have in varying degrees left their mark on other thirteenth century buildings in Ireland. Although the cathedral is only 212' (64.62m) long, unvaulted, and, as earlier writers have pointed out, is surpassed in size and splendour by many an English parish church, it is a uniquely impressive building. It has an austere beauty and, in spite of the fact that it is relatively small, it achieves a sense of monumentality. The lucidity of its overall design and the very high quality of its sculptural detail ensure its position as one of the finest medieval buildings in the country (Pl. I, *frontispiece*).

The cathedral, as it now stands, dates from the thirteenth century, but there is evidence of earlier building on the site. Unfortunately our knowledge of it is scanty and often circumstantial. The absence of annalistic evidence from Leinster compounds the problem: there is virtual silence in the remaining annals regarding Kilkenny throughout the early medieval period. There are two references to the burning of the monastery in 1085 and again in 1114. To judge from the evidence of the round tower, a feature generally associated with the more prestigious foundations, one can assume the existence of a fairly substantial monastic settlement from at least the eleventh century onwards. This assumption is strengthened by the choice of Kilkenny as the diocesan seat of Ossory at the Synod of Rathbreasail in 1111: all the other sees chosen were monasteries of importance with origins reaching back to the sixth and seventh centuries. Indeed, the association with St Canice would allow a foundation date in the sixth century for Kilkenny, although there is no archaeological evidence to support this.

There is however evidence of a structure dating from the mid-twelfth century. Excavations carried out in 1863 revealed the foundations of an earlier building to either side of the present choir. Unfortunately these were not adequately documented and reports were contradictory.

More concrete evidence is supplied by a few carved fragments which remain. Several of these are loose, now stored within the cathedral; two were re-used in the thirteenth century building. They consist of a voussoir with carved interlaced beasts, a base with a carved head built into the lower wall of the south transept, and several jamb fragments, one of which was incorporated into the arch of the east window of the north choir aisle. From the evidence of other Romanesque buildings it is most likely that these formed part of either a chancel arch or west doorway; the size and nature of the Kilkenny remains suggest the latter. These were the main focal points for decoration in Irish Romanesque churches and were often inserted into an earlier construction. There is no evidence to suggest that the church at Kilkenny was either large in size or complex in structure.

The quality of the carving is very good; it is bolder and in higher relief than that generally found in Romanesque Ireland, and the high standard is indicative of the status of Kilkenny at this period. The decoration recalls traditional Irish motifs (the rows of beading, the running foliage scroll which can be found at Freshford and Killeshin). It also shows knowledge of English work but one cannot stress this point since from Cashel (*c*.1127) onwards features of English Romanesque had been known to Irish carvers and were frequently incorporated into their work. Comparisons with other works would suggest a date of *c*.1150-1175 for these fragments.

The documentary evidence for thirteenth century Kilkenny is more plentiful, but there are no primary sources relating to the building of the cathedral. Traditionally this has been attributed to the mid-century episcopate of Hugh de Mapilton, who was termed *primus fundator* by a sixteenth century catalogue of the bishops of Ossory. This source has been shown by Carrigan[2] to be unreliable for the thirteenth century. On the evidence of other Anglo-Norman cathedrals in the country the most likely candidate for the initiation of the building campaign was Bishop Hugh de Rous, the first Anglo-Norman in the see. It was normal policy for the invaders to replace part or all of the existing cathedrals with larger and grander structures. This process was generally carried out during the term of office of the first English bishop, often shortly after his appointment. At Kilkenny, this would suggest a starting date sometime during the period 1202-1218.

It is important to relate these dates to the wider perspective of English developments. By 1200 the Gothic style was well established in England: Canterbury choir, arguably the first Gothic building in that country, had been begun in 1175. The 1180s saw the building of Wells and Glastonbury; the 1190s the choir of Lincoln Cathedral. The mature work of the Early English period, Salisbury Cathedral, the choirs of Pershore and Worcester, were all begun in the 1220s. By 1250, the 'traditional' starting date for St Canice's, Early English was on the wane in England and a new concept, Decorated, was taking over as the fashionable style.

In Ireland, where cathedral architecture had been behind developments elsewhere during the twelfth century, it was the arrival of the Anglo-Normans which finally brought Irish ecclesiastical architecture into line with that in England. As Roger Stalley has pointed out in his study of Christ Church Cathedral[3], a substantial portion of the invaders came from the Severn Valley and they brought with them English-trained craftsmen, new techniques and materials.

It was not, however, until the early years of the thirteenth century that the first fully Gothic cathedrals appeared: the choir of Waterford Cathedral (begun *c*.1210), the nave of Christ Church, Dublin, (begun *c*.1216) and the new cathedral of St Patrick's begun *c*.1225. All three projects show a marked knowledge of contemporary building in the West Country of England and all were up to date in terms of their overall design and detailing. They were all vaulted, had three storey elevations, while the two Dublin cathedrals had ambulatories at the east end.

Such complex plans proved too costly to emulate outside Dublin, although sculptural details could be and were copied. In the provinces, there were simply not the funds to build on such an elaborate scale. When one turns to Kilkenny Cathedral, which was built in one of the major Anglo-Norman towns, this shortage of cash is highlighted.

Plate I   View of St Canice's Cathedral in 1791
(from F. Grose, *Antiquities of Ireland)* vol. 1, (London, 1791))

THE THIRTEENTH CENTURY BUILDING

The plan of Kilkenny Cathedral is cruciform, with a crossing tower, an aisled nave of five bays, and a partly aisled choir (Pl. 11a). Two eastern chapels lead off the transept. Although the Lady Chapel is a later rebuilding, the original south chapel could well have matched that to the north. The resulting plan at the east was thus a series of square chapels *en échelon*. Such an eastern termination was not uncommon in England. It had its roots ultimately in Romanesque, but thirteenth century examples can be found at Lanercost Priory and Halesowen Abbey both in Worcestershire.

It was not a pattern found in Ireland; at least there are no extant examples. It can perhaps be related to the Cistercian east end which favoured a series of transeptal chapels seen, for instance, at Graiguenamanagh Abbey. However, one crucial difference is that the chapels in the Cisterican examples were all of equal length and not *en échelon*.

27

With an overall internal length of 212' (64.62m) and a width across the transepts of 117' (35.66m) the Cathedral is outstripped only by St. Patrick's, the largest medieval building in the country, which is approximately 286' (87.17m) in length. It is worth remembering, on the other hand, that the smallest English Cathedrals, Carlisle and Southwark, which measure 262' (79.86m) and 239' (72.8m) respectively, are on a par with St Patrick's. Of the larger cathedrals in that country, seven are over 500' (152.40m) in length, over twice the length of Kilkenny.

EAST END DESIGN

Within the cathedral there is a clearly discernible change in design between the eastern half and the nave, indicating that a new mason (or masons) was brought in at this point. Unfortunately there is no clearly visible masonry break between the two phases (such as occurs at Christ Church for instance) but a careful stylistic analysis of the fabric indicates that the eastern design included the choir, its aisles, the transeptal chapels and the lower parts of the transepts, including the entrance into the nave aisles. The east end design is patently earlier in date. Thus the cathedral was built from east to west, a common, although not invariable medieval practice. The earliest portions are the nine lancet windows at the east end of the chancel (Pls. 111(a), (c)). Those on the east wall are pointed, while those to the north and south are round-headed. The retention of this essentially Romanesque feature (which also appears on the north transept doorway) alongside the pointed arch is a feature of architecture in Ireland. *c.*1178-1230, but it predominantly occurred in building west of the Shannon It is not commonly found in Anglo-Norman building after *c.*1210: it was retained in some Cistercian building, for instance Graiguenamanagh Abbey, but it was rare in ecclesiastical architecture after this date.

There are traces of some Victorian restoration on the eastern lancets: portions of the rere-arches have been replaced and all the banded shafts are new. However the major part of the carving is original, and all but one of the capitals appear to be so. The windows are highly decorative: the mouldings are enriched with dog-tooth ornament and there are foliage bosses between each lancet. The foliage in the capitals is of the standard late twelfth-early thirteenth century design known as stiff-leaf. Individual capitals vary in design, but the proportions of all are elegant, the line uncluttered with the foliage following and emphasising the curve of the inverted bell. All but three of the twelve capitals have a further embellishment; on the lower half of the neck there is a delicate incised pattern of tiny blind arcading.

Precise parallels for these capitals are hard to find. The simple trefoil leaf with accentuated mid-rib is a common early thirteenth century form and represents an early stage in the evolution of stiff-leaf, as seen for instance in the roof bosses of the western transepts at Lincoln. If compared to work at St Patrick's choir or the nave of Christ Church the design at Kilkenny is conservative, there is an absence of movement, a lack of deep undercutting.

The eastern windows at Graiguenamanagh have been cited by more than one authority as the source for those at Kilkenny (Pl.111(b)). While superficially they appear to be similar, on close examination there are significant differences. Both combine round-headed and pointed lancets, but at the Cistercian abbey the combination occurs within the triplet itself. Overall the design is much less elaborate: the rere-arch mouldings are of quite a different and more simple pattern; there is no

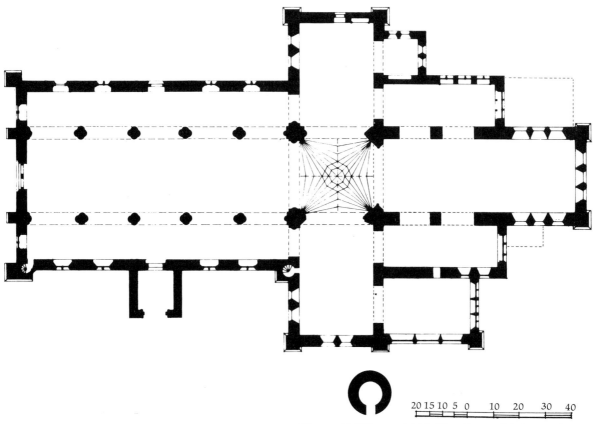

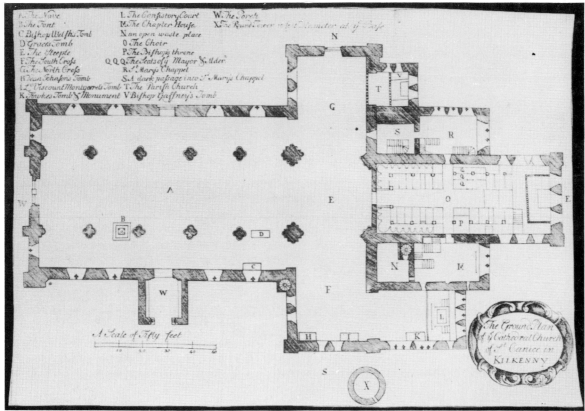

Plate II
(a) St Canice's Cathedral: Plan
(b) St Canice's Cathedral: Plan, 1791 (from Grose, *Antiquities of Ireland,* vol. 1)

dog-tooth ornament, no foliage bosses. Finally the majority of the capitals on these windows (and indeed throughout the abbey) are not of the stiff-leaf variety but are moulded. Where foliage capitals do occur (the two outermost on the east window) they are of quite a different pattern to those found at Kilkenny. In all, the similarities between the design of both windows are of too generalised a nature to indicate that the same group of masons was responsible.

More fruitful comparisons can be made between the chancel arcade at Kilkenny and the nave at Graiguenamanagh. Both arcades employ a square pier, with an intercolumniation of about 17' (5.18m). The moulding profiles of the arches are close. At the abbey the outer order of the arch moulding is not continued to the ground, but is terminated by a simple carving on the chamfered jamb. The inner order terminates in a corbel which is moulded with a line of ornament on the abacus. The corbels are badly damaged and have been broken away below the capital, but enough remains to show that they must originally have been akin to corbels on the choir arcade at Kilkenny which taper away below the capital. Such corbels are a common Cistercian type, occurring at Abbey Knockmoy and in the nave of Dunbrody Abbey. According to one source, the northern part of Graiguenamanagh was ready for roofing in 1228; though imprecise it most probably intends the north transept. It provides a rough indication for the chronology of the abbey, the nave of which must therefore date from the late 1220s or early 1230s.

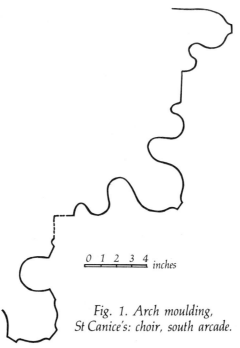

0 1 2 3 4 *inches*

Fig. 1. Arch moulding,
St Canice's: choir, south arcade.

There are several moulding profiles which occur exclusively in the eastern half of St Canice's. Such profiles can often assist in chronology. The most telling is the use of the triple filletted roll found on the choir arcade (Fig. 1), on an aumbry in the choir, and on the entrance from the transepts to the nave aisles. This profile occurs almost exclusively in Anglo-Norman buildings in Ireland and is most frequently found in the period *c.*1220 to *c.*1240. In England it became popular at a date nearer the mid-century,

Plate III
(a) East window,
St Canice's Cathedral
(b) East window,
Graiguenamanagh Abbey
(c) North Window,
Choir, St Canice's
Cathedral

but there are earlier examples at Lincoln Cathedral and St Alban's Abbey. The hollows on all the mouldings in the eastern part of the cathedral are deep, well formed, almost three-quarter circles, such as are not normally found before 1220 in England.

Plate IV   North Transept Doorway

Before leaving the choir design, there is one feature which must be noted; the north transept doorway (Pl. IV). Its design is unique and there are no obvious comparisons to be made with other Irish works. The two most unusual features are the banded roll continuous from jamb to arch, which forms the inner order of the doorway, and the foliage which was originally placed at intervals between the two rolls on the outer order, only small fragments of which remain. Large continuous convex rolls are a common Worcestershire type and can be found for instance at Worcester Cathedral and the parish churches at Bredon and Ripple. None of these is banded. The design of

32

the Kilkenny door has been compared to a doorway at the Cisterican abbey of Strata Florida in Wales. There, a series of continuous convex rolls are banded together at intervals by thin bands of masonry ending in spiral motifs. The rolls are unfilletted and the total effect is quite different. Closer parallels can be found in Scotland, where the large banded roll appears quite frequently, as at Kilwinning Abbey in Ayrshire, an early thirteenth century building, in a doorway leading from the nave to the cloisters, and at the west doorway at Arbroath Cathedral. Analysis of this doorway, of its moulding profiles and ornament, shows that it clearly belongs to the first phase of building.

The stylistic affinities between the choir arcade of Kilkenny and the nave of Graiguenamanagh would suggest a date in the 1220s for this area. On the other hand, the design of the eastern windows can be paralleled in the period 1210-1220. Taking all the evidence into account one can attribute the initiation of the building campaign to sometime before de Rous's death in 1218 or shortly afterwards. In other examples of Anglo-Norman rebuilding the new cathedral was generally begun soon after the appointment of the first English bishop. St Patrick's, Dublin was an exception. Although it was anglicised in 1191, the new work was not begun until 1225, due to a lack of funds which were being deployed in the building of the new nave of nearby Christ Church.

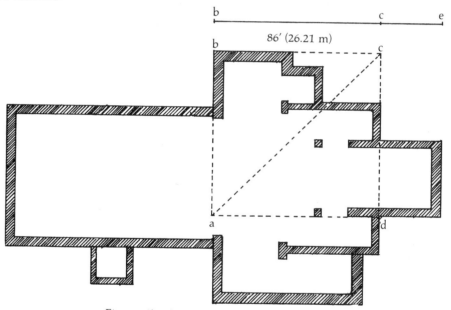

Fig. 2. Sketch plan showing proportional system.

PROPORTIONAL SYSTEM

There is evidence that the eastern parts were laid out with some care. The proportional systems used by medieval master masons have attracted much recent speculation. A popular working formula was 1: $\sqrt{2}$. In Cistercian building, on the other hand, a modular system of two related squares (generally in the ratio of 3:4) was widely used[4]. This has been shown to have been the case at Mellifont, Jerpoint, and Grey Abbey. At the last two the square of the cloister, a measurement of 100′ (30.48m), was taken as the starting unit. At Kilkenny, the main dimensions are governed by a square with a side of 86′ (26.21m) (Fig. 2). This has as its base line (ab), the western face of the crossing piers and the length of one transept. It thus defines the transepts, and the length of the choir aisles. The diagonal (ac), if rotated, gives the eastern extension of the chancel. The relationship of the length of the choir and crossing to the side of the square is thus 1: $\sqrt{2}$. The length (ae) (Fig. 2) is almost equal to the internal width across the transepts, that is 117′ (36.66m).

The side of 86′ determines the following dimensions:
1) divided by three this equals 28′8″ (8.74m), a dimension governing both the internal width of the choir and the internal width of the transepts
2) 28′8″ divided by two equals 14′4″ (4.37m), giving the internal square of the north chapel.

The distance from the eastern edge of the square to the chancel (ce) is 31′2″ (9.50m). Divided by two, this gives 15′10″ (4.83m), the breadth of the choir aisles. While the breadth of the nave was determined by that of the choir, its length does not bear any obvious relationship to it, reinforcing the conclusions already reached, that this area was laid out as a separate phase.

There are links with English works in the eastern design, some of which have their origin in the West Country. However the borrowings are generalised, such as might be picked up in Ireland itself by this date (at Christ Church for example, or at the many Cistercian abbeys under construction by the Anglo-Normans), although the design of the north transept door does not have any immediate prototypes. There is no strong evidence to suggest that the master mason was recruited directly from England. On the contrary the references to local Cisterican building suggest that his background and previous experience might have been in this area. Viewed in its entirety the design is accomplished and elegant in its detailing. It is, however, conservative and in some instances, particularly in the retention of the round arch, downright old-fashioned. This conservatism can perhaps be linked with the bishop during the period, Peter Malveisin (1221-1230) who, unlike his successors, was not a royal clerk and is not recorded as having travelled extensively.

As one might expect, the progress of the building was punctuated by periods of relative inactivity. The period 1232-1243 was one during which the see was neglected. While the dean and chapter were responsible for the day-to-day running of the building campaign, the job of raising the necessary funds generally fell to the bishop. Judging from what we know about the Bishop Walter de Brackley (who had to be reminded of his episcopal duties by the pope), and from the architectural evidence, it seems likely that progress slowed down during his term of office.

From 1244 to 1280, on the other hand, the see was occupied by men who had considerable experience in the service of the king, especially Geoffrey de Turville and Hugh de Mapilton. Both travelled frequently to England so that they would have been aware of architectural developments in that country. It is thus not too fanciful to relate the appointment of the first of these, de Turville, to the change in design apparent in the nave, and the engaging of a new master mason with a knowledge of a more-up-to-date design.

Plate V
(a) Nave, St Canice's
(b) Nave, St Mary's, Gowran
    (reproduced by kind permission of the Commissioners of Public Works, Ireland)
(c) Nave, Thomastown.
    (reproduced by kind permission of the Commissioners of Public Works, Ireland)

THE NAVE DESIGN

The change of style is clearly discernible in the nave arcade (Pl. V(a)); the piers, quatrefoil in plan, are widely spaced, the distance between them measuring on average 20'0" (6.25m). This is considerably wider than that found in either of the two Dublin cathedrals. A comparable width can be found at St David's in Wales which is also unvaulted; indeed such a wide span was possible only in a timber-roofed building. The shape of the piers is echoed in the clerestory windows, which visually integrates the elevation. In Ireland such a combination occurs only at the parish church at Gowran: so close are the overall architectural and sculptural links with this building that the mason of the Kilkenny nave has been described by one writer as 'the Gowran master'[5] (Pl. V(b)). Quatrefoil piers with the same wide stocky proportions are also found in the parish church at Thomastown, but there the clerestory is composed of a series of lancet windows (Pl. V(c)). Remains at Athassel Priory indicate that it also once had

35

quatrefoil piers in the nave arcade. A quatrefoil clerestory can be found at two Cistercian Abbeys, Hore and Bective, and in the choir at Cashel where they are given an idiosyncratic treatment typical of this building.

The quatrefoil pier is not an indigenous Irish feature: all indications are that it was first introduced into the country at Kilkenny. It is, on the other hand, quite commonly found in England in the thirteenth and fourteenth centuries, particularly in parish churches. Indeed, the form was not elaborate enough for the major buildings, although it could form the core of a more complex design, as in the cathedrals of Salisbury and Worcester. It occurs generally throughout the country, but with a high incidence in the West Country and particularly in Worcestershire, which suggests that the mason may have drawn his inspiration from this area.

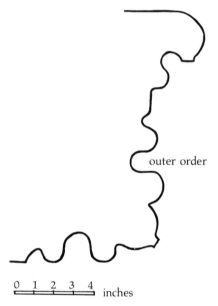

Fig. 3. Arch moulding, St Canice's: nave,
s. arcade 5th from east.

The moulding profiles of the arches also differ in the nave from those in the choir, again suggesting a change in master mason. A new profile appears towards the west end of the nave (Fig. 3) which can help to provide a termination date for this campaign. The profile occurs at Westminster Abbey *c.*1245, while comparisons with England as a whole indicate that although there are earlier examples it did not become popular until close to the mid-century.

In any discussion of the arch mouldings it is worth noting an economy of design which highlights the relative lack of funds available for building in the provinces in Ireland. The mouldings are not continuous from inner to outer order, the space between being filled with blank wall. A comparison with Christ Church, where they are carried unbroken across the arch, makes the point. Most of the large buildings in Anglo-Norman Ireland followed the Kilkenny pattern, but many were without moulded arches, being simply chamfered instead. Such was the case at Dunbrody Abbey, Gowran, and Thomastown. Thus moulded arches were in this country indicative of a certain status and were confined to the more important buildings.

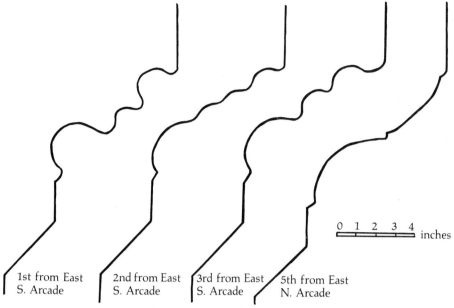

1st from East | 2nd from East | 3rd from East | 5th from East
S. Arcade | S. Arcade | S. Arcade | N. Arcade

0 1 2 3 4 inches

Fig. 4. Base mouldings: nave arcade.

A further clue to the dating of the nave is provided by the profile of the bases of the piers (Fig. 4). These are of a type known as roll bases and were the predominant form in England from *c.*1250 to 1290. In the choir the bases had all been of an earlier form known as waterholding (Fig. 5). However, these also appear on the nave doorways and on the arcade at Gowran. While the form was not totally discarded in England by 1250 (it can be found in the nave at Lichfield *c.*1260) its retention at the cathedral alongside the more up-to-date roll variety suggests a certain degree of anachronism on the part of the mason.

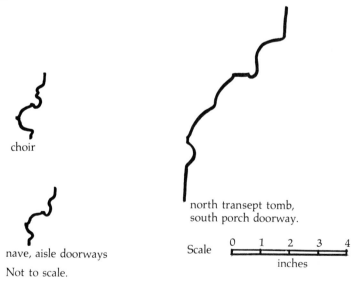

choir

nave, aisle doorways
Not to scale.

north transept tomb,
south porch doorway.

Scale   0   1   2   3   4
inches

Fig. 5. Base mouldings.

37

Plate VI
(a)   West doorway, St Canice's Kilkenny
(b)   West doorway, Wells Cathedral

WEST DOORWAY

The west doorway is quite clearly derived from that at Wells Cathedral, carved
c.1220 (Pls. VI(a), (b)). In both the main arch is subdivided, and the spandrel above has a
quatrefoil frame flanked by adoring angels on either side. The quatrefoil at Wells
contains a seated virgin and child; traces at Kilkenny suggest that it once contained a
similar piece.

The proportions of the Kilkenny door are broader and the advance in style and
decoration suggests a date *c*.1260. Overall, the design is more decorative. The arches
are embellished with cusping and the spandrel with a lavish use of foliage bosses which
however occur elsewhere at Wells Cathedral. In one instance the clarity of the original
has been lost in the borrowing: the angels have been reduced in size and placed within
quatrefoils: they become in effect a purely decorative motif. At Wells on the other

38

hand, they are an integral part of the composition, their bodies following and stressing the line of the arch, leading the eye towards the central figure.

Above the doorway is an unusual feature: three small openings give light to a small interior western gallery (Pl. VII). There are no extant examples of this feature in Ireland and it is a rare occurrence elsewhere.

Plate VII
Western Gallery, St Canice's

At Kirkstall and Fountains Abbeys in England there was a narrow gallery within the west windows, the function of which was to give access to the space between the vaults and the roof of the aisles. Clearly this was not the case at Kilkenny. Nor does the gallery facilitate access to the roof. The most likely explanation is that it served some liturgical function. Western doorways played an important ceremonial role in the middle ages: they formed the processional entrance and were only opened on the most prestigious occasions. They were also an integral part of the ceremonies of Palm Sunday. It is probable that at Kilkenny members of the choir were positioned in the gallery to greet the entrance of ceremonial processions. It is, however, a small and narrow space and would not comfortably accommodate more than three or four (small) choristers. The closest parallel, the western gallery at Arbroath in Scotland, is much larger, in effect a chamber.

Plate VIII
(a) Tomb recess, north transept, detail
(b) Label stop, west window, Gowran

THE GOWRAN MASTER

The master mason of the Kilkenny nave was without doubt one of the most gifted sculptors in thirteenth century Ireland. His work was largely confined to carving label stops and doorways, although evidence of his capabilities on a larger scale can be seen on the west doorway, while his ability to unite architecture and sculptural decoration can be seen perhaps most clearly in the nave of Gowran. Unfortunately most of his work at the cathedral was on the exterior and has weathered very badly indeed. Inside the church, however, there is a carved tomb recess in the north wall of the north transept, which happily has survived in relatively good condition (Pl. VIII(a)). It enables one to see clearly the characteristics of his style. The faces have full lips and chins, rather long noses, high eyebrows; a definite way of cutting the eyes with a flat lower lid and a high pointed upper one. There is an absence of any definite facial expression on the faces, which tend to be serene and somewhat idealised. The foliage used on the capitals is conventional and not particularly inventive, with a fondness for rosettes. Carved heads are found as label stops on all the nave doorways. Close examination reveals the same facial characteristics. There is a particularly fine group on the entrance to the south porch. By comparison with the heads on the tomb, these display greater touches of realism: a bishop on the east side has his cloak pulled tightly across his shoulders. The tendency towards a greater degree of realism can be seen in a very fine group of remarkably well preserved figures on the west window at Gowran

40

(Pl. VIII(b)), where there is a greater variety of facial expression. Several of the figures on the south porch wear brooches, as do many at Gowran. Further afield, brooches can be found on some of the carved heads at Christ Church and on figures at Wells and Lichfield cathedrals. Indeed, such carved heads are common enough in the architecture of the period. In Ireland other examples are found at Christ Church and Cashel. In England there are numerous examples: Wells, Worcester, Salisbury. Abroad, there are notable series at Rheims and Burgos cathedrals. Generally, they served a purely decorative function and were not intended to serve as portraits of anyone in particular. At Salisbury, on the other hand, a plausible case has been made for the heads representing a portrait gallery of those involved in the building of the cathedral. There is indeed a great variety of facial type. However, the frequent appearance of the same facial type at both Gowran and Kilkenny would indicate that this was not the case here, nor is there evidence of any iconographical programme behind their positioning.

By far the greatest number of heads at the two Kilkenny buildings depict males with short hair. These represented members of the clergy. Male laymen, by contrast, were generally depicted with longish hair, curled up at the ends, apparently reflecting a fashion in the thirteenth and fourteenth centuries for curling the hair with hot irons. All the women depicted wear the pillbox headdress typical of the period. There are in addition at the cathedral two bishops depicted. It is possible that they symbolised the founder bishop St Canice, or perhaps one of the thirteenth century prelates.

A further characteristic is the manner in which the carved heads alternate with foliage on several of the capitals at St Canice's and Gowran: on the tomb and south porch at the cathedral; and on a doorway, now blocked, in the tower at the parish church. The motif was popular in the West Country, originating in Wells Cathedral. It was introduced into Ireland at Christ Church and quickly spread down the south-east of the country (Fig. 5). It was a feature which could easily be copied, and, unlike stone vaulting, was not prohibitive in cost. It evidently appealed to local masons. In several instances such capitals were inserted into an existing building — as at Monaincha in Tipperary — no doubt with the intention of giving an up-to-date touch.

Fig. 6. Map showing the distribution of head and foliage capitals.

Details in the eastern end of the nave can be paralleled in works of the 1240s. A terminal date for the arcade is provided by a new moulding profile — a type popular from *c.*1250 onwards — which appears at the west end. The fully developed roll bases also support a date in the 1250s. An overall chronology of *c.*1245 to *c.*1265 for the nave is consistent with the evidence. The traditional attribution of the building to Hugh de Mapilton has thus some basis since the erection of the nave would have coincided with his term of office.

The source of many of the details of the mason's style has been shown to be in the West Country, in keeping with the pattern observable in Anglo-Norman building generally in Leinster. A distinction must be made, however, between Christ Church nave and Waterford choir, on the one hand, and Kilkenny on the other. The two earlier projects were begun in the first quarter of the century at a period when due to the lack of a tradition of large scale building, it was necessary to recruit masons from England. Thus both these designs are more firmly rooted in specific buildings. By the 1240s, however, there must have been a considerable number of masons already in the country and the need to recruit from outside would no longer have been as imperative. Moreover, by this date the first spate of building activity was over: it can hardly have been a lucrative proposition for a mason to come to Ireland to design what was by English standards a large parish church.

There is no concrete evidence to show that the Gowran master was recruited directly from England. Certainly he was aware of buildings in that country, but none of the models he used was particularly up-to-date. The Wells west doorway, for instance, was by 1260 over thirty years old. There is also a heaviness and a sense of mass and weight in the design of the Kilkenny nave which looks back to the period of High Gothic: each element of the design is clearly separated from the next; there is a concern for the plastic accentuation of the piers and arches which was essentially out of touch with contemporary architecture in England and France.

The old-fashioned elements in the design are symptomatic of the gradual isolation, at least in architectural terms, of the country as a whole. In building west of the Shannon a marked conservatism had always been a feature of design; the lingering on of Romanesque features up to and beyond the mid-century is evidence of this. In Anglo-Norman areas there is an equally apparent, although not so obviously pronounced, break with English developments. There had been a brief period in the mid-teens and early twenties when in the design of Christ Church and, to a lesser extent, St Patrick's, Irish buildings had actively contributed to the contemporary development of English Gothic. Outside Dublin, however, economic strictures, combined with the lack of incentive for foreign masons resulted in a stylistic divergence between Ireland and England, the proof of which is seen most clearly in the time-lag in the importation of new features.

INFLUENCE

Not surprisingly the new nave at Kilkenny seems to have exercised a considerable influence on building in the vicinity, for the Kilkenny workshop acted as an important source for the dissemination of ideas. Its impact can be clearly seen at Gowran where the advance in style would suggest a chronology of *c.*1260 to *c.*1275. The nave there is generally more decorative, while the very beautiful double window at the east end of

Plate IX
South aisle window, Gowran

the north aisle is more elaborate and ornamental than any found at the cathedral (Pl. IX). The lower half of the nave elevation at Thomastown drew heavily on the Kilkenny design, but here the cathedral was not the only source of inspiration, for one can detect the influence of other buildings in the area; the full extent of the Gowran master's direct involvement is subject to question. His style, however, can be seen at two other buildings in Kilkenny town. The choir of St John's Priory has on its east and south windows head and foliage capitals which clearly derive from those in the cathedral, although the dating is problematic: the priory was founded in 1202, but the Y tracing of the windows cannot date much before 1280.

The opening-up of the wall surface and the shifting of emphasis to the windows in St John's is reminiscent of the lady chapel at the cathedral, which is slightly later than the main body of the cathedral. That it was originally shorter in length can be seen in the south window of the choir aisle which is bisected by the east wall of the chapel. Comparisons with St John's would suggest a date in the 1280s. Both these examples reflect in a greater degree the new fashions in England.

Elsewhere, the influence of the Gowran master may be traced in the respond in the outer face of the north wall of the tower of the Franciscan friary in Kilkenny, where there was clearly a chapel or transept. At the base of the capital are two small heads which Leask, on the basis of the mouldings, dated *c.*1300. However, the capital is so similar to responds at Gowran that a date nearer 1270 would be more appropriate.

II

The visitor to Kilkenny cathedral today sees a building not very different in appearance to that which existed in the thirteenth century. True, the walls were unlikely to have been stripped of plaster, the choir would not have been open to the nave, and it is probable that the tower was of a different design. However, these differences aside, the cathedral is closer now in appearance to the medieval church than it was at any time during the period 1332-1870. Indeed the visitor in 1800 would have found a building considerably less well lit and open than it is today, and, one feels, rather gloomy: the choir, fitted with eighteenth century classical furniture, was cut off not only from the nave (by a solid screen wall) but also from its aisles, the latter being all but blocked by stairways giving access to the choir gallery. The southern aisle was partly unroofed and open to the weather. Most of the tall lancet windows east of the crossing were shortened or blocked up, while the Lady Chapel in particular was in a sad state. A visitor in the 1850s described it as 'the most doleful church imaginable'.[6]

MEDIEVAL RESTORATION

The greater part of the internal modifications, particularly those to the choir and aisles, resulted from the collapse of the crossing tower in 1332 which was recorded by the contemporary Kilkenny annalist, John Clyn, who must have observed its ruins:

> cecidit campanile sancti Kannici Kylkennie et magna pars chori, vestibulum capellarum, et campanas, et meremium confregit, die veneris, 11 kal. Junii; unde horribile et miserabile spectaculum erat contuentibus.

> (on Friday 22 May the belfry and a great part of the chancel of St Canice's, Kilkenny, collapsed, demolishing the entrance to the side chapels, the bells, and the timber work, a most terrible and pitiful sight to behold).[7]

The collapse of the crossing tower was a common failure in medieval buildings; numerous instances could be cited. It is difficult now to pinpoint the reasons for collapse, but at Kilkenny it was obviously thought that the tower buttressing was at fault: in the rebuilding the eastern crossing piers were enlarged, the choir arcades were blocked up, and a solid screen wall was erected at the west end of the choir. The result of these modifications can be seen in the Ware-Harris plan of 1798 (Pl. II(b)). The rebuilding of the damaged parts was carried out by Bishop Ledrede c.1354. He also built the new tower (a short stumpy affair) and erected the stained glass windows in the choir. These were greatly admired by the Papal Nuncio, Rinuccini, in the seventeenth century, but were destroyed by Cromwellian troops.

In the fifteenth century the splendid Lierne vault was erected over the crossing. By Irish standards it was a complex design and represented the culmination of a series of vaulting experiments in the Ormond area.

There were numerous reports of disorder and decay in the Irish church during the fifteenth century, which not unnaturally resulted in the gradual decay of many buildings. Kilkenny, however, seems to have been an exception, enjoying throughout the fifteenth and first half of the sixteenth centuries a good deal of prosperity. Neither the cathedral nor its environs was neglected: in 1597 the cathedral was reroofed, and in 1614 the steps and gate leading to it were erected. This concern for the upkeep of the fabric was in marked contrast to other cathedrals in the country: Christ Church and St Patrick's in particular suffered serious decay during this period.

The Architecture of the Cathedral

THE SEVENTEENTH CENTURY

The Cromwellian occupation of 1650 was the second serious threat to the fabric. Bishop Williams, returning to the cathedral after the restoration in 1661 gave a colourful description of the results:

> the great, and famous, most beautiful cathedral church of Saint Keney, they have utterly defaced, and ruined, thrown down all the Roof of it, taken away *five* great and goodly Bells, broken down all the windows, and carried away every bit of the Glass, that they say was worth a very great deal; and all the doors of it that Hogs might come, and root, and Dogs gnaw the Bones of the dead.[8]

The same source reveals that destruction was not confined to Kilkenny and that the fate of St Canice's was only part of a campaign of destruction throughout the country. In England, particularly in the counties held by the parliamentary forces, the damage inflicted was generally far greater.

Whatever the damage to St Canice's it must have been repaired by 1672, for the earliest extant chapter book dates from then and it contains no reports of any substantial repairs being necessary. Indeed the earliest entries indicate that the cathedral was whitewashed and new flags were laid in 1673, neither of which tasks could have been carried out in a derelict building. Accounts show the cathedral to have been kept in fairly constant repair by a body of permanent workmen employed by the chapter throughout the seventeenth and eighteenth centuries.

EIGHTEENTH CENTURY RESTORATION

In 1756 Richard Pococke, a keen antiquarian and experienced traveller, was consecrated bishop of Ossory. According to his biographer he found the cathedral in a considerable state of decay. However this is contradicted both by the chapter accounts and by the fact that most of Pococke's projects were concerned with beautifying the church rather than with any structural repairs.

His major task consisted of 'improving and adorning the inside of the choir' by means of new fittings and furniture. From surviving letters it is clear that he played a key role in the design of these. The most significant aspect is that they were to be carried out in a Gothic style. Interest in this style was in the mid-eighteenth century confined to a small body of *cognoscenti*, of whom Pococke was one. However his letters reveal that in common with most of his contemporaries his knowledge and understanding of Gothic was only superficial (which was not helped by the paucity of published material on the subject), and he viewed it primarily in terms of its ornament. For instance, in relation to a new bishop's seat he wrote: 'if the Pillars . . . consist of four members that will give it a Gothic look'[9]. In the end the choir furniture was executed in a classical style, employing a Greek Ionic order. While this was greatly criticised by nineteenth century writers, it was by no means uncommon: both Winchester and Worcester were among the many English cathedrals to receive such a treatment; in Ireland, some years earlier, a similar compromise had been reached at Waterford cathedral which, ironically, had been severely criticised by Pococke. Indeed had his original designs been carried out, they would have afforded a very rare example of eighteenth century ecclesiastical Gothic, since its application at this period was largely confined to secular buildings. The work on the choir was completed by 1762, the materials of the old choir furniture being given to the bishop to dispose of as he thought fit.

Pococke also built a colonnade leading from the north transept doorway to the Bishop's House. He organised the repositioning of the monuments which had been strewn about the cathedral since the Cromwellian occupation. Finally, he authorised the blocking up or shortening of windows, particularly at the east end. Once again, it is worth noting that this was not unusual, as a study of both Ely and Peterborough cathedrals will show. It was probably a measure of economy.

In 1765 Pococke was translated to the diocese of Meath. On his departure he was formally thanked by the dean and chapter 'not only for the ornamenting but almost the very being of our Cathedral'[10].

NINETEENTH CENTURY RESTORATION

Several reports on the fabric during the early years of the nineteenth century reveal that the cathedral had fallen into disrepair. Some repairs were carried out in the 1840s and 1850s, but these were minor in nature; it was not until 1863 that the restoration proper was begun.

The nineteenth century was the great period of church restoration; from the early 1840s until the late 1870s there was scarcely a major cathedral or important parish church in Ireland and England which escaped restoration — often necessary to prevent collapse — too frequently overdrastic in execution. There had of course been restorations in the preceding centuries, but these were not inspired by the deliberate and conscious desire to reveal the original design — or often what the restorers imagined to be the original design — which distinguished the nineteenth century approach. The mid-century marked the high point of the Gothic Revival and witnessed the elevation of medieval architectural styles (and indeed the middle ages as a whole) to an almost fanatical level. Under the influence of groups like the Ecclesiologists strict rules governing church restoration were drawn up and enforced. All classical furniture was zealously removed and all portions of the fabric which did not conform to the prevailing concept of the true Gothic style were demolished and rebuilt. At Christ Church, Dublin, for instance, George Edmund Street pulled down the fourteenth century choir, replacing it with his — at times fanciful — version of the original Romanesque design.

The architect appointed to the Kilkenny restoration in 1863 was Thomas Newenham Deane. A comparatively young man (*b*.1828), he was the son of the Cork architect Sir Thomas Deane and a founder member of the firm of Deane and Woodward, which spearheaded the Gothic Revival in Ireland. Their work was secular and heavily influenced by the writings of John Ruskin, whose approval they earned in designing the Museum Building in Trinity College, Dublin. In 1861 Deane became involved in his first work of restoration, Tuam Cathedral, which was completed by 1865 and received favourable reports in the *Dublin Builder*. He was therefore relatively inexperienced when he was approached by the Kilkenny chapter, but was the only architect of any note involved in restoration work in Ireland at this time. No doubt the high reputation of his architectural practice secured him the job.

He submitted plans for the restoration of St Canice's which, after some discussion by the restoration committee, were approved, and an estimate of £7,880, later amended to £10,000, was agreed. Work began early in 1864. By 2 August 1870 the main job had been completed and the cathedral was reopened for worship. During this period the building was entirely reroofed, the choir and aisles were cleared of Pococke's furniture, the blocked up arches were all opened, the lady chapel dismantled and carefully rebuilt reusing the original stones.

The restoration was on the whole a sympathetic one, concentrating only on restoring or replacing those portions which were necessary for the stability of the fabric. The medieval stone was treated with respect; there was, for instance, no attempt made to replace any of the weathered sculpture around the doorways. By nineteenth century standards, in the language of Ecclesiology which classified restorations as 'conservative', 'destructive', or 'eclective', this was a conservative approach, although in any assessment it must be remembered that the cathedral presented relatively few problems to the restorer. It was built in a uniform style. It was neither in a dangerous state of decay nor had any of it collapsed.

In only two respects did Deane deviate from his conservative policy. The castellation over the aisle walls had not existed previously, but in his designs for the roofs in the choir and nave he allowed himself greater licence. The magnificent hammer-beam designs were not only out of place within the context of an Early English building, but were not a feature of medieval Irish architecture, although there are plenty of examples to be found in England. It must be admitted however that they were a successful addition: visually they are very impressive and add interest and complexity in the nave to the somewhat austere perspective. Other aspects of the restoration were common to all nineteenth century work and were alien to thirteenth century practice. Chief among these were the opening up of the vista from choir to nave and the removal of the internal plaster to expose the rubble masonry.

The course of the restoration was not altogether a happy one: relations between the architect and the cathedral authorities became strained and there were a number of conflicts. The most serious arose as a result of problems with the roof which had begun to leak as early as 1865 and continued to do so despite the best efforts of the architect. In addition, the original estimate of £10,000 proved inadequate, for which Deane was blamed. In a letter to the chapter he rather bitterly commented 'I hoped to have pointed to it as a successful restoration carried out from my designs and under my supervision'[11]. He eventually resigned in May 1870, but his experience at the cathedral did not adversely affect his career as a restorer. On the contrary, he was appointed the first superintendent of the newly formed National Monuments Section of the Commissioners of Public Works in 1874. He made careful surveys of the buildings in his care and his reports are evidence of sensitive and conservative views on restoration.

Although the bulk of the restoration was completed by 1870, work continued into the 1890s under the direction of a local architect, Richard Langrishe. George Edmund Street was consulted in 1876 but seems to have done very little. All that can be attributed to him with certainty is the screen in the south choir aisle. Langrishe was responsible for the design of the interior of the south porch and for fittings in the lady chapel.

The cathedral has been fortunate in its history. Damage was repaired quickly, and since none of the changes made over the centuries was of a structural nature they could be undone in the nineteenth century. Alone among Irish cathedrals the basic fabric of St Canice's has remained largely unaltered.

A Worthy Foundation

FOOTNOTES

1. Anon., *A tour through Ireland in several entertaining letters by two English gentlemen,* (Dublin, 1764), p. 117.
2. W. Carrigan, *The history and antiquities of the diocese of Ossory,* (Dublin, 1905), i, pp. 28-9.
3. R.A. Stalley, 'The Medieval Sculpture of Christ Church Cathedral Dublin', *Archaeologia,* cvi (1979), pp. 107-22.
4. R.A. Stalley, 'Mellifont Abbey: a study of its architectural history', *R.I.A.Proc.,* lxxx (1980), Section C, p. 346
5. R.A. Stalley, *Architecture and sculpture in Ireland 1150-1350,* (Dublin, 1970), p. 75.
6. George Edmund Street in the *Irish Builder,* (April 1 1866), p. 82.
7. Editor's translation. Dr. Empey also suggests that the word *meremium,* which has been translated broadly as 'timber work', may here mean scaffolding, particularly if it is a Latin rendering of the medieval French *merrain* (bois de construction). In this case the tower may either have been in the last stages of completion, or else its condition was already cause for concern before the disaster. On the other hand, *meremium* could mean a wooden screen or perhaps the choir stall, or both. (R. Butler (ed.), *The annals of Ireland by Friar John Clyn and Thady Dowling,* (Dublin, 1849)).
8. Griffith Williams, *Seven treatises very necessary to be observed in these very bad days etc.* (London, 1661), Prefactory remonstrance.
9. November 3rd 1756. Reproduced in M. McCarthy, 'Eighteenth century cathedral restoration. Part II', *Studies,* lxvi (1977), p. 66.
10. Chapter Book I, 1672-1775, June 13, 1765.
11. Chapter Book III, 1850-1869, February 26, 1867.

GENERAL NOTE ON SOURCES:

The best general introductions to the period are H.G. Leask, *Irish churches and monastic buildings,* ii (Dundalk, 1955), and R.A. Stalley, *Architecture and sculpture in Ireland 1150-1350,* (Dublin, 1971).

On St Canice's cathedral, the only published work is the splendid monograph by J. Graves and J.G.A. Prim, *The history, architecture and antiquities of the cathedral church of St Canice, Kilkenny,* (Dublin, 1857). A more recent study is an unpublished M. Litt. thesis by S. Barry, 'Kilkenny cathedral: a study of its architecture' (Trinity College, Dublin, 1983).

For the later history of the fabric the minute books of the cathedral chapter contain a wealth of information.

The Medieval Tombs of St Canice's Cathedral

JOHN BRADLEY

St Canice's Cathedral is a beautiful expression of Gothic style conveying dignity, elegance and simplicity to the viewer. On first stepping into the cathedral most visitors look up at the mouldings of the nave arcade, the hammer-beam roof, the unique west window, the delicate vaulting of the crossing tower, the great lancets of the choir and transepts. This has often puzzled me for the building is not a high one. It is as if the firm verticality of the lancet windows acts subliminally to draw the eyes upwards towards heaven. If they look down, as often as not it is to avoid tripping over awkward stones protruding from the floor. Yet these stones form a most outstanding series of memorials, remarkable both in quality and quantity. In fact, the medieval burial monuments of St Canice's constitute the largest and most important single collection in the country.

Like the building these monuments have had a chequered history. Some of the memorials noticed in the cathedral during the early seventeenth century are now lost, but even more surprisingly some of the monuments described just over one hundred years ago by Graves and Prim are also missing.

The middle ages cannot be noted as a time when care was lavished on monuments. If the descendants of a dead person were unwilling or unable to maintain the memorial it would gradually fall into disrepair and eventually be removed or broken up. Two hundred yards away in the Dominican friary, for instance, a series of medieval tombslabs were broken up and reused as building stones during the construction of its west tower in the fifteenth century (Bradley 1980, 12:33-8). Tombslabs were also occasionally reused in making new memorials. The fourteenth century monument to John de Karlell (no. 16, below) was appropriated for use in 1612 as the tomb of Bishop Richard Deane. The plain slab commemorating Henry Blund (no. 17) was reset as the front panel of Bishop Walshe's altar tomb in 1575 (no. 58). The cross slab of Nicholas Motyng (no. 53) was built into the Renaissance style mural tomb of the Murphys in the 1640s. It is impossible to gauge how many memorials have been lost or broken up in this haphazard way but the greatest catastrophe in the history of the monuments was undoubtedly the Cromwellian sack of the cathedral in 1650. Bishop Griffith Williams wrote of it as follows in 1661:

> '. . . and they brake down a most exquisite Marble Font (wherein the Christian's Children were regenerated) all to pieces, and threw down the many *many* goodly Marble Monuments, that were therein, and, especially, that stately and costly Monument of the most honourable and noble Family of the House of Ormond, and divers others, of most rare and excellent Work, not much inferiour (if I be not much mistaken) to most of the best (excepting the King's), that are in Saint Paul's Church or the Abby of Westminster.' (Graves and Prim 1857, 43).

It was not until one hundred years later that anything was done to repair the monuments. Walter Harris, who visited the cathedral about 1739, saw the effigies and inscribed monuments piled up in the chapel on the north side of the chancel:

> 'wherein are several curious old Monuments of Men in Armour and other Stones, which are parts of Antient Monuments, lying loose against the Wall. It is a pity they are not refixed and preserved.' (Harris 1764, i, 434).

It seems reasonable to assume that the fragments which had survived the Cromwellian pillage had been collected together here. In 1763 Bishop Pococke commenced the repairing and arrangement of these monuments and an inventory, stating their location, was made for him by John O'Phelan, a local schoolmaster. The effigial monuments were carelessly reassembled and Pococke has been criticised for separating the tombs of Piers Butler and his wife Margaret FitzGerald (no. 41) and for placing the tomb frontal of Richard Butler (no. 55) beneath the effigy of Piers Butler. These inaccuracies were corrected in 1854, however, by the marquis of Ormonde who gathered the Butler monuments into the south transept. Graves, writing in 1857, laments the condition of the monuments at that time and rather pointedly states that they could be re-arranged and safeguarded for about £20. Twelve years later, in 1869, the decision to re-arrange was taken and Graves supervised the task, setting out the monuments in the location which they have had to this day. Since 1869, however, a number of additional pieces have come to light as a result of digging in the graveyard and Deanery garden.

Study of the Monuments

The earliest notice of monuments in the cathedral is by James Ware, writing in 1665, who describes the thirteenth century tombs of Bishops Hugh de Mapilton and Geoffrey St. Leger, both apparently in the south transept, and the tombs of Bishop O'Hedian, near the west door, Thomas Barry, David Hacket, and Oliver Cantwell, all of which are now lost. Ware (1665, 144, 149) also notes the tombs of Bishops Richard de Ledrede (no.13), Christopher Gafney (no. 57) and Nicholas Walsh (no. 58), and the slab which commemorates Bishop Richard Deane (no. 16). The inventory of the monuments prepared for Bishop Pococke in 1763 by John O'Phelan included thirty-five inscriptions of pre-1600 date. These were published by the antiquary Edward Ledwich in 1781, and again without alteration in the second edition of his *Antiquities of Ireland,* published in 1804. In 1813 O'Phelan's manuscript was the basis of a book on the tomb epitaphs written by Peter Shee, a native of Irishtown. Although useful in some respects, Shee's book is poor on the whole. His transcriptions are inaccurate and while Ledwich published thirty-five medieval inscriptions, Shee could only muster thirty from the same manuscript. However Shee added two additional tombs (nos. 57 and 60), one of which (no. 57) was seen by Harris about 1739 and was strangely overlooked by O'Phelan. Indeed neither Ledwich nor Shee did full justice to O'Phelan's original work and it remained to James Graves and John Prim to use it fully in their history of the cathedral published in 1857. In this monumental work they described fifty-seven medieval tombs adding nine new inscribed monuments and detailing twelve uninscribed tombs for the first time. In the restoration of 1863-70 a number of slabs were found and Richard Langrishe, the architect responsible for some of this restoration work, listed sixty-seven medieval monuments in 1879. The additions comprised four inscribed stones and seven uninscribed tombs. The total of inscribed monuments now stood at forty-eight, and the uninscribed totalled nineteen. However, one of the slabs listed by Graves and Prim (no. 88) is noted by Langrishe as missing, although he actually confused it with no. 29 commemorating a person with the same name. P. M. Egan gave a list of monuments in his *Guide to Kilkenny* (1884) but it was derived from Langrishe, and like the lists that have appeared in subsequent guides, it was also selective. Canon Carrigan in his diocesan history of 1905 added two new inscribed tombs. Since that time another monument has been lost (no. 88) while a number of new slabs and fragments have come to light. In 1966 Edwin Rae published a study of the tomb of James Schortals (no. 33); Mrs Phelan (1969) has made a general survey of the occurrence of apostles on Ossory tombs; and in 1974 John Hunt described the effigial tombs and the decorated tomb-fronts and end panels, publishing seven of them for the first time. Today, there are eighty-one medieval monuments in the cathedral or its immediate vicinity, but since Langrishe's time no full listing has been attempted. The aim of this section is to redress that situation by giving a complete list of the extant medieval monuments, a brief commentary on each and a general discussion of the tombs themselves.

Dating the tombs

The medieval tombs of St Canice's range in date from the thirteenth to the sixteenth century and are particularly important because so many of them can be closely dated. Thirty-three have inscriptions providing a date: two in the thirteenth century, another two in the fourteenth, and twenty-nine in the sixteenth century. In other cases the inscription gives the name of the commemmorated individual but not the date, and occasionally it is possible to identify the figure historically and assign a date to the tomb if the year of the person's death is known. Four of the fourteenth- (nos. 13-16) and one of the fifteenth-century tombs (no. 27) may be closely dated in this way. The remaining monuments are more broadly dated: the uninscribed effigial tombs on the style of costume and the cross slabs on the basis of their similarity to examples which can be closely dated. This similarity may be based on the form of slab, the shape of the cross, or the style of the inscription. It is fortunate that the effigial memorials have been the subject of a major study by Hunt (1974), on which I have drawn considerably. Of these, one may belong to the late thirteenth century (no. 4), five date from the fourteenth century (nos. 5-6, 18-20), and two from the sixteenth (nos. 43, 47); in addition the side panels of altar tombs, both those lying loose (nos. 73-80) and those reset under effigies (nos. 33, 41, 43, 47, 49, 62) may also belong to the sixteenth century (with the exception of the end panel of no. 41, which appears to be of seventeenth century style). The solitary stone sarcophagus (no. 26) can only be assigned a very broad thirteenth-fourteenth century date, the period when this type of memorial was in fashion (Bradley in press).

Of course one should not automatically accept the date of death as the year in which a tomb was made. The standard practice during the middle ages was for individuals to commission a tomb while they were still alive, generally on the practical grounds that if it was left to their heirs they would be reluctant to spend much money on it. St Canice's has many examples of tombs put up before their patrons died, particularly during the sixteenth century. The effigy of James Schortals (no. 33), for instance, was commissioned in 1507 but he was still alive in 1534; similarly the effigy of John Grace (no. 49) bears a date of 1552 whereas he did not die until 1568. Indeed a glance at many of these tombs (e.g. nos. 37, 39-41, 44-45, 50, 52) will reveal blanks for the day, month and year of death of the commemorated person, which have never been filled in, presumably because the heirs did not bother to employ a mason. No. 41, the effigy of

51

Margaret FitzGerald, is the strangest of these because the mason was obviously employed to do the job but put in only the day and month of death and omitted the year!

In terms of numbers the sixteenth century is the best represented with fifty-nine extant and three missing tombs (nos. 33-81, 87-89), the fifteenth century has the least with only one definite example (no. 27) and three missing (nos. 84-6). The thirteenth century has two surviving and two lost slabs (nos. 1-2, 82-3) and the fourteenth century has twelve (nos. 5-7, 12-20) but there are eleven monuments which could be either thirteenth or fourteenth century in date (nos. 4, 8-11, 21-26) and five which could belong to the fourteenth or fifteenth century (nos. 28-32).

Form

The material of the tombs is almost entirely local limestone and these were presumably made in or near Kilkenny. The names of two of the sixteenth century masons are preserved on the tombs: Rory O'Tunney (no. 49) and William O'Tunney (no. 50), members of a family of sculptors that is traditionally associated with Callan (Hunt 1950, 23). No. 11 may be Caen stone, and no. 25 appears to be slate; these may have been imported in a complete state. Graves and Prim (1857, 129-30) describe two fragmentary brass matrices of uncertain date but their whereabouts is now unknown. Only three of the medieval tombs appear to be in their original position (nos. 39, 57 and 58). The others have all been relocated. In particular, the side-panels of the altar tombs have been reassembled and it is difficult to reconstruct their original form, except in the case of no. 33 which has been studied by Rae (1966).

The tombs show interesting changes in the fashion of burial monuments between the thirteenth and sixteenth centuries. In general terms a change of fashion is most marked between the sixteenth century and the preceding centuries but distinctions can also be seen between the memorials of the thirteenth, fourteenth and fifteenth centuries. These general changes may be summarised as follows. During the thirteenth and fourteenth centuries burial monuments tended to be recumbent slabs placed on the ground, characterised by a coffin-shape (i.e. trapezoidal) and decorated with a fleur-de-lis cross. Inscriptions are brief and occur in Lombardic lettering. Latin is the usual language but Norman-French occurs in two instances (nos. 2, 12). Tomb-form was not stereotyped, however, and even in the fourteenth century a diversity is apparent. Effigial slabs, both incised and relief, are present (nos. 4-6, 13, 18-20), although elsewhere in Ireland these are known from the thirteenth century. Rectangular slabs, plain except for an inscription, are a characteristic tomb type of the fourteenth century (nos. 3, 7, 16, 17), and in the latter half of the century a distinctive type of eight-armed cross-head makes its appearance and continues into the early years of the fifteenth century (nos. 12, 15, 27, 28, 31, 32). The coffin-shaped slab also begins to fade out during the fourteenth century and the tomb of Robert Ferr (no. 3) marks the first appearance of the rectangular slab which was to replace it. On the tombs of John and Richard Talbot (nos. 15, 27) the coffin shape has become a mere taper. Blackletter script also begins to appear towards the end of the fourteenth century on tombs such as those of William Carleil (*d.*1384), John Talbot (*c.*1385) and John de Karlell (*d.*1394) and eventually it completely replaced the Lombardic script. The fifteenth century is the one least well represented at St Canice's, but what there is suggests that the styles established by the end of the fourteenth century continued into the fifteenth. During the sixteenth century elaborate altar tombs with an effigy supported on decorated side panels appear. These are cenotaphs and elsewhere in

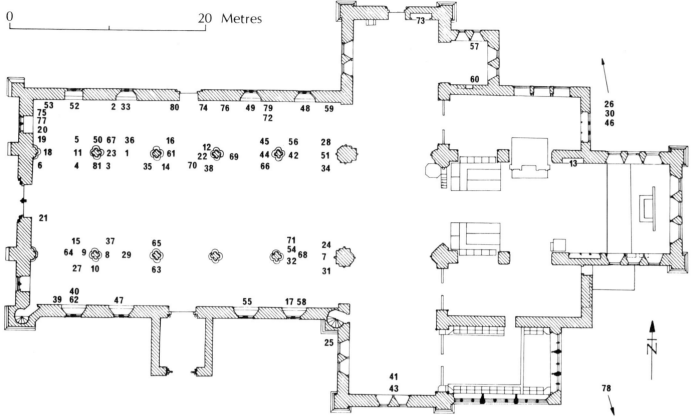

Fig. 1. Location plan of monuments.

Ireland they commence in the late fifteenth century. New styles of cross-slab become common: segmental, intricately interlaced, and banded, almost all rising from a stepped base representing Calvary. The instruments of the Passion are also common decorative motifs and some slabs are decorated with these symbols alone. The inscriptions too become much more elaborate, indulgences are granted, and prayers and meditations are recited. Slabs also frequently function to commemorate many generations of the same family. Mural plaques, a standard form of seventeenth century memorial, make their first appearance with the Bourcier monument of 1584 (no. 59).

Social Information

The tombs provide a useful insight into the social history of medieval Kilkenny. The commemorated individuals are usually churchmen, merchants or members of the professional classes, and just as there was a social hierarchy in life, so the magnificence or simplicity of the tombs reflected that hierarchy continuing into death. The broadest social spread is seen in the sixteenth century with the elaborate effigial tombs of great landed proprietors like the Butlers, Graces and Schortals clearly portraying their former social status in the resplendence of their attire. By contrast, the altar tomb of Bishop Nicholas Walsh is plainer and much less lavish, and the tombs of other

53

churchmen such as John Moghlande (no. 34) and Robert Gaffney (no. 60) are mere floor slabs. Edmund Purcell, a captain of the earl of Ormond's troops, is shown in armour on his slab, sharing it with the instruments of the Passion. Merchant families such as the Cotterells, Lawlesses, Pembrokes, Donoghues, and Savages are also commemorated by floor slabs, some with delicately interlaced crosses, others with a simpler combination of spiritual motifs. There are no memorials to artisans, labourers or peasants among these tombs and obviously the cost of commissioning one was beyond their reach and also, perhaps, their aspiration. There is, however, one late sixteenth century tomb to a tradesman, Donatus Brin, who would appear from the tools depicted on his tomb (no. 69) to have been a carpenter. Coming as it does at the end of our period it has a singular importance: the sole bluecollar in a whitecollar world. In its own unobtrusive way it is an indicator of the beginning of the social changes which were to create our modern world.

Catalogue

In the following inventory description is kept to a minimum. The slabs are all of fossiliferous limestone, unless stated otherwise. The inscriptions are given as they appear on the tombs and the medieval contractions are not expanded. Readers who wish for the extended Latin text are referred to earlier authors. Where letters appear in square brackets these are supplied from Carrigan unless stated otherwise. With modern typesetting it is not possible, without enormous expense, to show the various different forms of contraction used during the middle ages and strokes above letters, for instance, have been omitted. However, whatever letters appear on the tomb are given below.

1. Henry de Ponto of Lyra. 1285x8
Fragmentary slab, probably rectangular originally, decorated with a shield in relief and bearing an incised Lombardic inscription:

> +HIC IACET: . . . . .C:M. . . . .[LIUS: HENRICI: DE: PONTO: DE: LYRA: QI: OBIIT: IN: DIE: DE]COLLACOIS: BI: IOHIS: BAPTISTE: ANNO: DNI: M: CC: LXXXV. . .

> Translation: Here lies . . . . . son of Henry de Ponto of Lyra who died on the feast of the Decapitation of Blessed John the Baptist [29 August] A.D. 128[5x8]

The portion of the inscription within brackets has been missing since Carrigan's time and is supplied from Graves and Prim. Nothing is known of Henry de Ponto. His name may be derived from Drogheda which is named in a number of early thirteenth century documents as Ponte (bridge); to a lesser extent the name was also applied to New Ross. Graves and Prim suggested that Lyra may be Lyrath, near Kilkenny, but as the name appears to be derived from Lee's rath (Graves and Prim 1857, 148, note a) this explanation is unlikely.

Graves and Prim 1857, 142-3:1; Langrishe 1879, 13:1; Carrigan 1905, iii, 149:1.

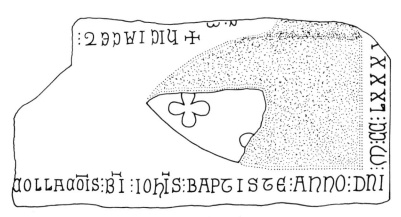

Fig. 2. No. 1: Henry de Ponto of Lyra. 1285x8.

2. Joseph de Keteller. 1285x8

Coffin-shaped slab with bevelled edges, decorated with an incised fleur-de-lis cross down the centre and marginal Lombardic inscription in Norman-French:

> +: ICI: GIST: JOSE: DE: KETELLE[R]: D.RE:.E: DIST: TV: KI: CI: VAS . . . .
> TRESPASA: LAN: DE: GRACE: MIL: E: CC: E: QVATRE: VINS: . . .

> Translation: Here lies Joseph de Keteller. Say (a prayer) you who pass by . . . died in the year of Grace 128[5x8].

The slab was discovered in High Street in 1894 during renovation work on the building now occupied by O'Neill's Pharmacy and the Kilkenny People offices. It led to speculation at the time that there had been a church in this vicinity. However, it seems far more likely that the slab had simply been reused for building purposes. It was moved here from St Mary's Church in 1952. The family of Keteller was settled in Kilkenny by the end of the thirteenth century and gave their name to 'Kyteler's Inn', mentioned in Kilkenny Corporation documents as Kyteler's Hall from the fifteenth century. In 1302 William Kiteler was sheriff of the Liberty of Kilkenny. Their most celebrated member was Alice Kyteler, tried for heresy and sorcery at Kilkenny in 1324.

Egan 1895; Carrigan 1905, iii, 102.

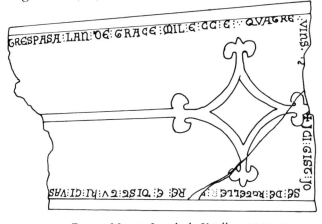

Fig. 3. No. 2: Joseph de Keteller. 1285x8.

3. Robert Ferr. 1300.
Rectangular slab with slight bevel along the sides. Marginal inscription in incised Lombardic letters:

> + HIC IACET: ROBERTVS FERR A [..O D M CCC] OBIIT...PAT: ET AVE COT[I]DIE [O]MNI[B.S PRO A]IA DICENTIBVS...[N...IA DIERVM].

> Translation: Here lies Robert Ferr. He died [in A.D. 1300]. An indulgence of . . . days will be granted] to all who daily say an Our Father and Hail Mary [for his soul].

Graves and Prim 1857, 147-8:7; Langrishe 1879, 13:7; Carrigan 1905, iii, 151:7.

Fig. 4. No. 4: Head-slab of a priest (?). Late 13th/Early 14th cent.

4. Head-slab of a priest (?). Late 13th/Early 14th cent.
Rectangular and plain except for a sunken head carved in false relief. Prominent ears with a bold roll around the forehead, perhaps representing a tonsure. The date is based on English parallels cited by Hunt.

Langrishe 1879, 12:B; Hunt 1974, 183: no. 134.

56

Fig. 5. No. 5: Head-slab of a man. Early 14th cent.

5. Head-slab of a man. Early 14th cent.

Coffin-shaped with bevelled edges. Ornamented with an exuberantly decorated fleur-de-lis cross rising from a stepped base. Above the cross are the worn head and shoulders of a man, his head resting on a rectangular pillow and his hair curling below the ears, a style in vogue shortly after 1300.

Graves and Prim 1857, 133-4; Langrishe 1879, 11:E36; Hunt 1974, 184: no. 136.

Fig. 6. Fourteenth century incised slabs: Nos. 6, 18-20.

6. Incised slab of a woman. Early 14th century.

Fragmentary. The woman wears a gown tightly fitted at the neck with full sleeves falling beyond the elbow. Below this the closely fitted sleeves of the kirtle extend to the wrist. Her hands are raised and spread outwards on her breast. The date is suggested by the style of dress.

Graves and Prim 1857, 133; Langrishe 1879, 11:E35; Hunt 1974, 184: no. 136.

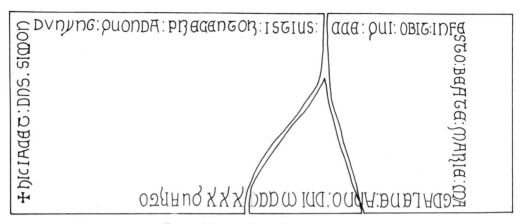

Fig. 7. No. 7: Simon Dunyng. 1334.

7. Simon Dunyng. 1334.

Rectangular slab. Unornamented except for an incised marginal inscription in Lombardic lettering:

> + HIC: IACET: DNS: SIMON: DVNYNG: QVONDA: PRECENTOR: ISTIUS: [E]CCE: QUI: OBIT: IN: FESTO: BEATE: MARIE: MAGDALENE: ANNO: DNI: M: CC[C]: XXX: QUARTO.

> Translation: Here lies Master Simon Dunyng; formerly precentor of this church, who died on the feast of Blessed Mary Magdalen [22 July] 1334.

The Dunnings were prominent in Kilkenny during the late thirteenth and early fourteenth century. Alan Dunning is the earliest known sovereign (a position known today as mayor) of Kilkenny, an office which he held on at least four occasions in 1293, 1295, 1305, and 1312. Although Simon Dunning's name survives as the witness of a number of charters, little is known of his life. He appears to have been appointed precentor *c.*1304.

Ledwich 1781, 467; Shee 1813, 47; Graves and Prim 1857, 146-7:6; Langrishe 1879, 13:6; Carrigan 1905, iii, 151:6; Leslie 1933, 73.

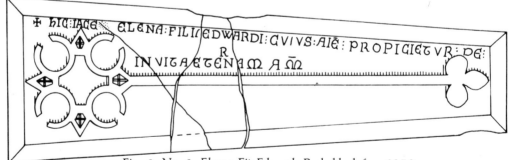

Fig. 8. No. 8: Eleana FitzEdward. Probably before 1350.

8. Elena FitzEdward. Probably before 1350.

Coffin-shaped slab with bevelled edges. Ornamented in relief with a cross terminating in expanded fleur-de-lis terminals springing from a trefoil at the base. Incised

Lombardic inscription in two lines along the sinister side of the cross:

+ HIC: IACET: ELENA: FILIA: EDWARDI: CVIVS: AIE: PROPICIETVR: DE:
IN VITA: ETERNAM: AM

Translation: Here lies Elena FitzEdward on whose soul may God have mercy
for life eternal. Amen.

Nothing is known of Elena FitzEdward and the slab is assigned to the thirteenth-
fourteenth century on stylistic grounds. The fine Lombardic lettering and the well-
defined colons between the words would suggest that the slab is not later than 1350.

Ledwich 1781, 397; Shee 1813, 47; Graves and Prim 1857, 144-5:3; Langrishe 1879,
13:3; Carrigan 1905, iii, 150:3.

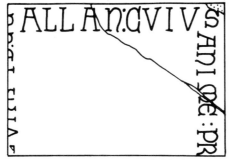

Fig. 9. No. 9: Allan slab. Probably before 1350.

9. Allan slab. Probably before 1350
Rectangular fragment with incised Lombardic inscription:

. . . . ALLAN: CVIVS: ANIME: PR . . .

Translation: [Here lies] . . . allan on who soul [may God have mercy].

A number of letters have been partially cut off before the initial A; these could be read
as . . lundi de C[allan], suggesting perhaps a member of the Blund family. The date is
assigned to this slab on the same basis as No. 8.

Graves and Prim 1857, 145-6:5; Langrishe 1879, 13:5; Carrigan 1905, iii, 150:5.

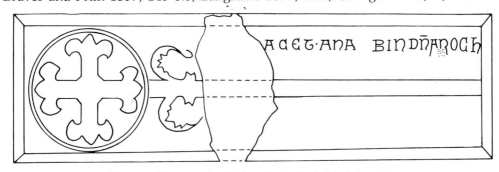

Fig. 10. No. 10: Anabindna Roch. Probably before 1350.

10. Anabindna Roch. Probably before 1350.
Rectangular slab with bevelled edges. The base has been chiselled-off in modern times.
Ornamented with an incised fleur-de-lis cross set within a ring; two serrated leaves

spring from the shaft below the ring. Incised Lombardic inscription:

... ACET ANABINDNA ROCH

Translation: [Here] lies Anabindna Roch

Nothing is known of the person commemorated but a date can be suggested on the same basis as No. 8. The slab bears a second incised inscription in blackletter of sixteenth century date: HIC IACET, written as if it were a test or trial piece.

Langrishe 1879, 13: 3a; Carrigan 1905, iii, 150:3a.

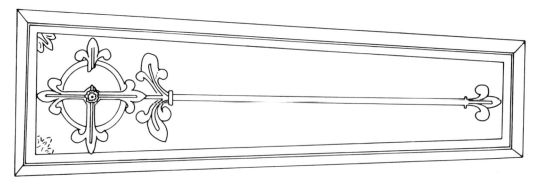

Fig. 11. No. 11: Uninscribed. Probably before 1350.

11. Uninscribed. Probably before 1350.
Coffin-shaped with bevelled edges. Caen stone(?). Ornamented with a floriated cross in relief. The edge is defined by a roll-moulding. The date is suggested on the basis of style and material.

Langrishe 1879, 12:A.

Fig. 12. No. 12: Lyuns slab. Mid 14th cent.?

12. Lyuns Slab. Mid 14th cent.(?)
Rectangular fragment bearing an eight-armed interlaced cross-head with fleur-de-lis terminals. Incised Norman-French inscription in Lombardic lettering:

.... E: LYVNS: G[IS]T: ICI: DEV: DE: SA: ALM....

Translation: Here lies .... e Lyuns on whose soul may God [have mercy].

The family of Lyons are well represented in fourteenth century Kilkenny and appear as burgesses in the *Liber Primus Kilkenniensis*.

A floral design ornaments the centre of the cross-head. The similarity of the cross design to that on nos. 15 and 27 would suggest that this slab belongs to the late fourteenth or early fifteenth century. However, the presence of an inscription in Norman-French written in Lombardic script indicates that it is unlikely to be so late. A date in the mid-fourteenth century may be proposed.

Graves and Prim 1849, 145:4; Langrishe 1879, 13:4; Carrigan 1905, iii, 150:4.

Fig. 13. No. 13: Richard de Ledrede. 1360.

13. Richard de Ledrede. 1360.
Reset into a niche in the chancel north wall *c.*1870 the piece is well-finished on the dexter side only and was meant to be seen from that viewpoint. Hunt points out that its present position is unlikely to be its original one because ecclesiastics were buried with their head to the east whereas in this instance the head points to the west. Ware,

61

however, states that the tomb was on the north side of the high altar.

The effigy is well carved in high relief and shows the bishop mitred and dressed in the normal pontificalia for the mass, holding a crozier in his left hand and with his right raised in blessing. Instead of wearing shoes, however, he is shown with the open-toed sandals of a Franciscan friar. The effigy is identified as that of Ledrede because he is the only known Franciscan to have been bishop of Ossory during the middle ages.

Richard de Ledrede had a long and chequered career as bishop from his consecration at Avignon in 1317 until his death in 1360. He figures prominently in the documentary sources as a pursuer of heretics, most notably in the notorious trial of Alice Kyteler in 1324. His reformer's zeal and overbearing nature made many enemies and consequently he spent much of his episcopate outside of Ireland.

Ware 1665, 144; Graves and Prim 1857, 132; Hogan 1874-9; Langrishe 1879, 11:E34; Carrigan 1905, i, 45-57; Leslie 1933, 6-8; Hunt 1974, 184-5: no. 140; Neary 1984.

14. William Carleil. 1384.
Coffin-shaped slab badly fragmented into eight pieces. It is plain except for its inscription which is incised in blackletter. Attractive floral designs are placed between the words CARLEIL and QOND, and between YOCHIL and AC.

> HIC [IACET DN]S WILLMS CARLEIL QoND' RECTOR DE YOCHIL AC ARCHIDIACON' MID' & ECCLIAR' DUB[LI]NES' CASS' OSSOR' FERN' CLON' & CORKAG' CANONIC' & . . . . CUI' AIE PPICIET' D'S AM

> Translation: Here [lies Master] William Carleil, sometime rector of Youghal, also archdeacon of Meath, and canon of the [cathedral] churches of Dublin, Cashel, Ossory, Ferns, Cloyne and Cork, and . . . . on whose soul may God have mercy. Amen.

William Carleil is known to have been active in the king's service from 1364 until his death on Ash Wednesday 1384. He was a collector of debts in 1364 but by 1372 he had become second baron of the exchequer in these latter functions he was also a member of the king's council. In 1383-4 he is listed as William Carlele, chaplain, among the burgesses of Kilkenny. From the documentary references it would appear that most of his attention was devoted to royal business and the long list of benefices on this tomb would seem to have been one of the perks of the job.

Ledwich 1781, 467; Shee 1813, 46; Graves and Prim 1857, 151-5:9; Langrishe 1879, 13:9; Carrigan 1905, iii, 151:9.

15. John Talbot, c.1385.
Rectangular slab. Ornamented with an incised but extremely worn eight-arm interlaced cross with fleur-de-lis terminals, very similar to nos. 12 and 27. The inscription, incised in a combination of Lombardic and blackletter, is placed along the sinister side of the cross:

> + HIC IACET IOHES TALBOT CUI' AIE PPICIET' DS.

> Translation: Here lies John Talbot on whose soul may God have mercy.

Although this slab does not bear a date, Graves and Prim have suggested that the John Talbot it commemorates is to be identified with a man active in Kilkenny during the mid- to late-fourteenth century. He is first referred to as sheriff of the Cross of

Fig. 14. No. 15: John Talbot. c.1385.

Kilkenny when he rendered the accounts for the years 1334-1340. In 1357 he was one of the portreeves of Kilkenny and he is last mentioned in 1381. His death can probably be placed shortly after this time.

Ledwich 1781, 477; Shee 1813, 68; Graves and Prim 1857, 148-51: 8; Langrishe 1879, 13:8; Carrigan 1905, iii, 151:8.

Fig. 15. No. 16: John de Karlell. 1394.

16. John de Karlell. 1394.
Fragmentary slab. Probably rectangular originally, now broken into three pieces. Marginal inscription in incised blackletter:

> HIC IACET DNS JOHES DE KARLELL Q[oN]DA CANCELLARIU[S] ECC
> .... [SANCTI] PATCII DUBLIN' AC ECCLIARU FERN' & LYM'ICEN'
> CANOIC' & ....

> Translation: Here lies Master John de Karleil sometime chancellor of the church .... [of St.] Patrick, Dublin, also canon of the [cathedral] churches of Ferns and Limerick, and ....

John de Karlell was a brother of William commemorated in no. 14. He also pursued a career in the government service and was one of the barons of the exchequer in 1391. He died on the feast of St Michael the Archangel [29 September], 1394.

The slab was reused in the seventeenth century when the coat of arms of Richard Deane and the following blackletter inscription were added in false relief:

[HI]C JACET RICHARDUS DEANE NUPER EPUS OSSORIENS' Q .... 20 DIE MENSIS FEBRIARII ANNO DNI 1612

Translation: Here lies Richard Deane, late bishop of Ossory, who [died] 20 February 1612.

The year of his death by our calendrical reckoning was in fact 1613. Deane was a Yorkshireman, appointed dean of Ossory in 1600 and bishop in 1610.

Ware 1665, 149; Harris 1764, i, 420; Ledwich 1781, 478-9; Shee 1813, 72; Graves and Prim 1857, 155-8:10; Langrishe 1879, 14:10; Carrigan 1905, iii, 152:10; Leslie 1933, 16.

17. Henry Blund. 14th cent.
Plain rectangular slab reused as the front panel of the tomb of Nicholas Walshe (no. 58). Incised Lombardic inscription running parallel to one of the long sides:

HIC IACET HENRICUS BLUNDUS

Translation: Here lies Henry Blund

He was presumably a member of the le Blund family of Callan, one of whom, Adam le Blund, was married to Alice Kyteler c.1302. The fashion for plain slabs bearing only the name of the deceased seems on the basis of nos. 7, 14 and 16 to have been a fourteenth century phenomenon.

Bradley 1980, 16:59.

18. Incised figure of an ecclesiastic. 14th cent.
Fragment, showing only the upper part of the body and lacking the head. He is wearing a low-necked gown with wide sleeves. The strap of a mantle is visible beneath the neckline. His hands are placed palm outwards on his chest. The date is suggested on the basis of the gesture of the hands and the costume.

Graves and Prim 1857, 134; Langrishe 1879, 12:E38; Hunt 1974, 184: no. 137.

19. Incised figure of an ecclesiastic. 14th cent.
Fragment missing the head and lower part of the body. The figure is shown wearing the amice and chasuble with the hands outspread in an identical gesture to no. 18. Hunt suggests a late fourteenth century date on the basis of the vigour of the incision.

Graves and Prim 1857, 135; Langrishe 1879, 12:E39; Hunt 1974, 184: no. 138.

20. Incised fragment. 14th cent.
This consists of the feet of a man wearing pointed shoes; just above the ankles is the lower part of what may be an alb decorated with a diamond pattern. The date is suggested on the basis of its comparison with nos. 18-19.

Graves and Prim 1857, 133; Langrishe 1879, 11:E35; Hunt 1974, 184: no. 139.

21. Rosia Bul. 13th-14th cent.
Fragment with incised Lombardic inscription and the arc of a ringed cross:

[+ HIC] IACET: ROSIA: [BVL] .... ANIME PROPIC [IETVR: DS]

Translation: [Here] lies Rosia Bul [on whose] soul [may God] have mercy.

The portion of the inscription within brackets is missing from before Carrigan's time and is supplied from Graves and Prim who note that in 1417 a Thomas Bull of Foulkstown held a garden within St Patrick's Gate. The style of lettering suggests a thirteenth/fourteenth century date and this Thomas may have been a relative or descendant of Rosia. Ledwich, however, gives the name as Rosia Ruu.

Ledwich 1781, 466; Graves and Prim 1857, 144:2; Langrishe 1879, 13:2; Carrigan 1905, iii, 150:2.

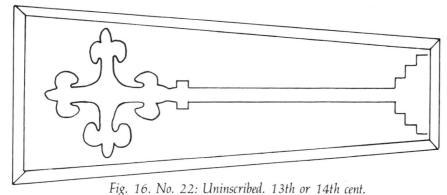

Fig. 16. No. 22: Uninscribed. 13th or 14th cent.

22. Uninscribed slab. 13th or 14th cent.
Coffin-shaped with bevelled edges. Decorated with a fleur-de-lis cross set on a stepped base.

Langrishe 1879, 12:D.

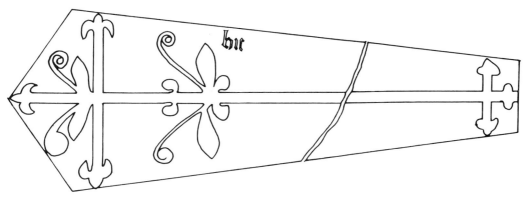

Fig. 17. No. 23: Uninscribed. 13th or 14th cent.

23. Uninscribed slab. 13th or 14th cent.
Coffin-shaped slab with bevelled edges. Worn fleur-de-lis cross with foliate stem in false relief. The head is pointed rather than flat so that the overall shape is pentangular. The word HIC is incised in sixteenth century blackletter along the sinister side of the cross.

Graves and Prim 1857, 134; Langrishe 1879, 11:E37.

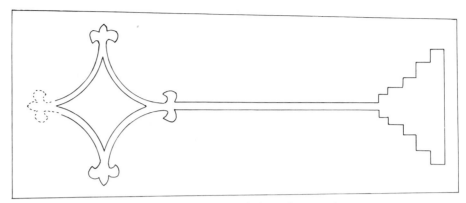

Fig. 18. No. 24: Uninscribed. 13th or 14th cent.

24.   Uninscribed slab. 13th or 14th cent.
Rectangular slab with incised fleur-de-lis cross rising from a stepped base.

Langrishe 1879, 12:F.

25.   Uninscribed slab fragment. 13th or 14th cent.
Beside the west wall of the south transept, on the exterior, is a small fragment of a floor slab decorated with the terminal and portion of the shaft of a fleur-de-lis cross. Its material appears to be slate.

Bradley 1980, 16: no. 60.

26.   Stone sarcophagus. 13th-14th cent.
Placed against the north wall of the churchyard with the sinister side partly buried. Penannular head with pillow. Curved shoulders. Two soakage holes. A narrow ledge runs around the outline of the body.

This sarcophagus would originally have had a covering slab but none of the monuments at present in the cathedral would appear to fit. Only sixteen such sarcophagi are extant in Ireland. They date from the thirteenth and fourteenth centuries.

Bradley in press, no. 6.

27.   Richard Talbot, c.1410.
Tapering slab ornamented with an incised eight-armed interlaced cross-head with fleur-de-lis terminals but lacking all trace of a shaft. Worn blackletter inscription incised along edge:

> H[IC IACE]NT RICARD' TALBOT QUONDA BURGE[N]S VILLE KILKE .... AIE PPIC .... [E]N [PATER ET] AVE MARIA:

> Translation: Here lie Richard Talbot sometime burgess of the town of Kilkenny .... [and .... on whose soul may God have mercy. Amen. An Our Father and] Hail Mary.

Graves and Prim suggest that Richard was a brother of Robert Talbot who 'built' the walls of Kilkenny in 1400, according to Stanihurst. Richard is mentioned on a number of occasions in the *Liber Primus Kilkenniensis*, 1407 being the latest date. It would appear

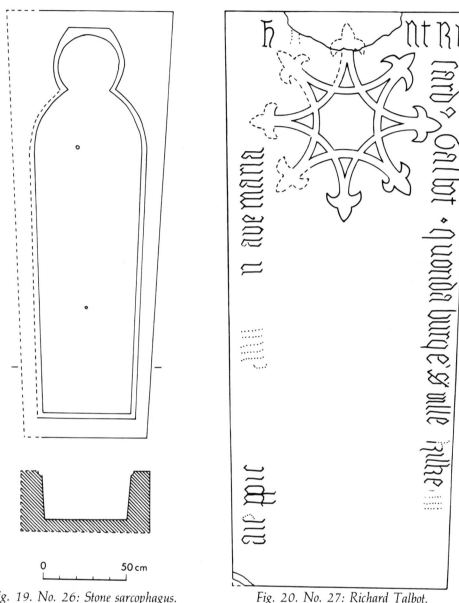

Fig. 19. No. 26: Stone sarcophagus.
13th or 14th cent.

Fig. 20. No. 27: Richard Talbot.
c.1410.

that he died shortly after this and Graves and Prim suggest 1408 as the year of his death.

Graves and Prim 162-3:12; Langrishe 1879, 14:12; Carrigan 1905, iii, 152:12.

28. Richard Forstall. Late 14th or early 15th cent.
Coffin-shaped slab with incised eight-armed interlaced cross-head with fleur-de-lis terminals rising from a stepped base. A bulbar expansion along the shaft encloses a quatrefoil. Incised inscription in blackletter:

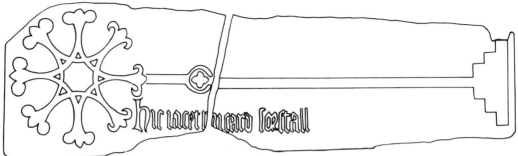

Fig. 21. No. 28: Richard Forstall. Late 14th/Early 15th cent.

HIC IACET [R]ICARD FORSTALL

Translation: Here lies Richard Forstall.

Ricardus Forstall is mentioned on the roll of burgesses of Kilkenny for the year 1383-4. The cross is comparable in style to nos. 12, 15 and 27.

Graves and Prim 1857, 104-5: 13; Langrishe 1879, 14:13; Carrigan 1905, iii, 152:13.

Fig. 22. No. 29: William Vayl. Late 14th or 15th cents.

29. William Vayl. Late 14th or 15th cent.
Fragment of a limestone slab with an incised inscription in blackletter:

HIC IACET DN' WILLMUS VAYL . . . .

Translation: Here lies Sir William Vayl . . . .

The family of De Valle or Wall has been in Co. Kilkenny since the thirteenth century. Graves and Prim suggest that this may be the memorial of a William de Valle who was active in Carlow and Kildare during the mid fourteenth century and is last mentioned in 1359. This identification cannot be made with certainty, however, and although the undecorated form of the monument could indicate a fourteenth century date the blackletter inscription suggests that it could equally well have been erected in the fifteenth.

Graves and Prim 1857, 158-62:11; Langrishe 1879, 14:11; Carrigan 1905, iii, 152:11.

30. Phillip Bryk. Late 14th or 15th cent.(?)
Fragment lying against the north wall of the churchyard and partially buried in earth.

It bears traces of a cross shaft. Incised blackletter inscription:

[.... IPP' BRYK CUI' AIE PPICIE]T' DEUS. AMEN.

Translation: [Here lies Phillip Bryk on whose soul may] God [have mercy]. Amen.

The missing letters are supplied from Carrigan.

Carrigan 1905, iii, 172.

31. Uninscribed. Late 14th or 15th cent.
Fragmentary slab with tapering sides suggesting that it was originally coffin-shaped. Decorated with an incised eight-armed cross with fleur-de-lis terminals rising from a stepped base similar in style to nos. 12, 15 and 27.

Langrishe 1879, 12:G.

Fig. 23. No. 32. Uninscribed. Late 14th or 15th cent.

32. Uninscribed. Late 14th or 15th cent.
The cross-head of a slab similar to no. 31.

Langrishe 1879, 12:E.

33. James Schortals and Katherine Whyte. 1507.
Altar tomb. Armoured effigy on mensa. The side panels, decorated with saints, are not the original ones. The figure is wearing overlapping plates above a skirt of mail on the body. The arms and legs are protected by hinged plates with cowters at the elbows and poleyns over the knees. The hands are gauntleted and the feet are shod with pointed sabatons, resting on a lion. The neck and shoulders are defended by a pisane, pointed

over the chest with besagews on the shoulders. The head-piece is a bascinet. The sword is hung from a belt at the waist. The head rests upon a cushion flanked by the Arms of the Passion on the dexter side, and on the sinister a cross with five lions heads caboshed upon it. Marginal inscription in blackletter:

> HIC IACET JACOB' SCHORTHALS DNS DE BALYLORCA & DE BALYK'F' Qi HAC TUBA FIERI FECIT ANO Di M CCCCC VII. ET KAT'INA WHYTE UXOR EI' P' QUOR' & PARETU' AIAB' CiLIBET [D]. . . . DINca. & SALUTAe' AGL' COCEDUT LXXX DIES INDULG'.

> Translation: Here lie James Schortals, lord of Ballylarkin and of Ballykeefe who had this tomb made in 1507. And Katherine Whyte his wife. An indulgence of eighty days is granted to those who say the Our Father and Hail Mary for their souls and the souls of their parents.

The tomb was commissioned during the lifetime of James Schorthals. He was still alive in 1534 when he is described as being about seventy years of age. Presumably he died shortly after.

The tomb front shows six figures in niches: SS Peter, Paul, James Minor, Thomas, Bartholomew and John. Dr Rae has shown that the original side panels of this tomb were nos. 74, 75, part of no. 41 below and a piece now in the National Museum of Ireland.

Ledwich 1781, 469; Shee 1813, 51; Graves and Prim 1857, 165-73: 14; Langrishe 1879, 14:14; Carrigan 1905, iii, 152:14; Rae 1966; Phelan 1969, 63-4; Hunt 1974, 185-6: no. 141.

34. John Moghlande. 1508.
Rectangular slab with banded and interlaced cross-head in relief. Marginal blackletter inscription continued on the cross:

> HIC IACET MAGR JOHES MOGHLANDE QUODA CANCELLARIUS OSS' ECCLIE QUI OBIIT XIX DIE MESIS MARCII ANNO DNI M CCCCC VIII P' CUI' AIA CVILIB' DICETI PTR' NR & AVE M' 'CEDUT' A REVEDO PRE OLIV'O [EPO OSS] XL DIES IDVLG'.
> QUISQS ER' Q' TNSIER STA P'LEGE PLORA' SM QD ER' FUERAQ' Q' ES P' ME P'COR ORA.

> And on the base:
> JOHES MOGHLANDE DE MONTE.

> Translation: Here lies Master John Moghlande, formerly chancellor of the [cathedral] church of Ossory who died 19th March 1508. An indulgence of forty days is granted by the Reverend Father Oliver, [bishop of Ossory] to those saying an Our Father and Hail Mary for [the repose of] his soul.
> Whosoever passes, stand, read, lament. I am what you shall be. I was what you are. Pray for me, I beseech you. John Moghlande of the Mountain.

The Moghlandes or Mullins lived in Kilkenny during the fourteenth and fifteenth centuries and are occasionally mentioned in the civic records.

Ledwich 1781, 466; Shee 1813, 45; Graves and Prim 1857, 173-5; Langrishe 1879, 14:15; Carrigan 1905, iii, 153:15.

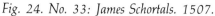

Fig. 24. No. 33: James Schortals. 1507.

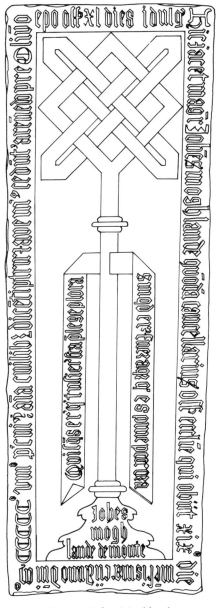

Fig. 25. No. 34. John Moghlande. 1508.

35. Peter Grant. 1510.

This slab is now almost totally worn and can only be identified because it is shown on the location map published by Langrishe in 1879. It had an eight-armed segmental cross with fleur-de-lis terminals rising from a stepped base, and a marginal inscription in raised blackletter read by Carrigan as follows:

HIC IACET PETRUS GRANTE QUODAM DN' DE RA .... AN, COR ....
ET BALLET .... IT DIE XXV MENS' .... BRIS .... CCCC X CUI' AIE
PPICIET' DE' AMEN.

71

Translation: Here lies Peter Grant, formerly lord of Ra[thKyr]an, Cor[luddy] . . . . and Ballyt[arsney], who died . . . .ber the 25th, 1510. On whose soul may God have mercy, Amen.

In the eighteenth century O'Phelan read this inscription as commemorating Peter Grant, vicar of Ballytarsna and student of Oxford. The cross is similar to nos. 39 and 42.

Ledwich 1781, 464; Shee 1813, 43; Graves and Prim 1857, 175-7:16; Langrishe 1879, 14:16; Carrigan 1905, iii, 153-4:16.

36. Inscribed Fragment. 1512.
Lower part of a coffin-shaped slab with faint traces of an incised cross set on a stepped base. Marginal blackletter inscription in false relief:

> . . . . I CANICI KILKENIE [QUI] OBIIT XXVII DIE MESIS SEPTEBRIS ANNO DNI M CCCCC XII CUI AIE PROPICIETUR . . . .

> Translation: . . . . of [St] Canice, Kilkenny, [who] died on the 27th September 1512. On whose soul [may God] have mercy . . . .

Ledwich 1781, 479; Graves and Prim 1857, 178:17; Langrishe 1879, 15:17; Carrigan 1905, iii, 154:17.

37. Thomas Power et al. 1519 et seq.
Rectangular slab with a worn eight-armed interlaced cross in relief with fleur-de-lis terminals. Blackletter inscription:

> IHS. HIC IACET THOMAS POWER Qi OBIIT ANNO DNI M CCCCC XIX. ET MARGERIA PYNSO UXOR EIUS. JOHES POWER FILIUS ET HERES DICTI THOME CU SUA UXO[RE] JOHANA SAWADGE Q OBIERUT ANNO D. M.CCCC. QUIQUAGESSIO. RICUS POWER EIUS JOHIS FILIUS ET HERES QUONDAM BURGENSES VILLE HIBERNICE KILKENIE QUI RICUS OBIIT 27 DIE MENSIS MAII A DNI M CCCCC 83. ET ISABELLA ROTH UXOR ILLI' Q OBIIT [   ] DIE MENSIS [   ] A DNI M. CCCCC [   ].

> Translation: Jesus. Here lies Thomas Power who died in 1519. And Margaret Pynson his wife. John Power son and heir of the said Thomas with his wife Johanna Sawadge who [both] died in 1550. Richard Power, son and heir of the said John, formerly burgesses of the Irishtown of Kilkenny; which Richard died the 27th of May, 1583. And Isabella Roth, his wife, who died the [   ] day of the month of [   ] A.D. 15[   ].

The Powers are referred to in civic records from the fourteenth century. Of the individuals listed here, Richard Power is mentioned on a number of occasions in the Corporation Book of Irishtown (*Analecta Hibernica* 28 (1978), 1-78). The cross-head is similar to no. 54.

Ledwich 1781, 464; Shee 1813, 44; Graves and Prim 1857, 178-9:18; Langrishe 1879, 15:18; Carrigan 1905, iii, 154:18.

38. Thomas Karroke. 1520.
Tapering slab ornamented with a cross fleurée in false relief rising from a graduated base. Marginal blackletter inscription:

Fig. 26. No. 38. Thomas Karroke. 1520.

HIC IACET THOMAS KARROKE Qi OBIIT XXVI DIE MES' JULII ANNO DI M CCCCC XX. CUI' AIE P'PICIETUR DEUS. AMEN.

Translation: Here lies Thomas Karroke who died 26th July 1520. On whose soul may God have mercy.

Nothing is known of Thomas Karroke.

Ledwich 1781, 479; Shee 1813, 75; Graves and Prim 1857, 179-80:19; Langrishe 1879, 15:19; Carrigan 1905, iii, 154:19.

39. Thomas Myghel et al. 1528 et seq.
Plain altar tomb in its original position. Segmental cross, banded with blackletter inscription in false relief:

OMNIB' ORAE' DiNCAM CU SALUTACONE ANGELICA P AIAB' REV'ENDI PRIS DAVID DEI GRA EPI OSS AC MRI THOME MYGHEL UT' USQ' IURIS BACCALARII OFFIlis OSS' AC ISTI' & CASS' ECCIAR' CANOci Q Hc IAC' AC THOME HAKKEDE BURGES' VILLE KYLKE'II DEVOn' DICETIB' TOCIES QCIES CCCC DIES IDULGECIE 'CEDUNT'. HIC IACET NICHOLA' HAKHED QUODA BURGES VILLE KYLKENIE' FILIUS & HERES P'FATI THOME HAKHED Qi OBIIT [   ] DIE MES' [   ] ANNO DOMINI MILLISIMO CCCCC XX [   ]. ET MARGARETA ARCHER UXOR EIUSDE NICHI Q OBIIT XXIX DIE MES' APiLIS A.D. M CCCCC XXVIII QoR' AIAB' P'PICIET' DE' AE.

Translation: An indulgence of four hundred days is granted to all persons each time they devoutly say an Our Father and Hail Mary for the souls of the Reverend Father David by the grace of God bishop of Ossory, and of Master Thomas Myghel, bachelor of both laws, official of Ossory and canon of this church and of Cashel; and also of Thomas Hakkede burgess of the town of Kilkenny, who lie here.
Here lies Nicholas Hakhed, formerly burgess of the town of Kilkenny son and heir of the aforesaid Thomas Hakhed who died on the [   ] day of the month of [   ] A.D. 152[   ]. And Margaret Archer, wife of the same Nicholas who died 29th April A.D. 1528. On whose souls may God have mercy. Amen.

73

This tomb would appear to have been erected by Nicholas Hacket on the death of his wife in 1528. David Hacket was bishop of Ossory from 1460 to 1478 and would appear to have been a relative. Thomas Mighell is referred to among the Ormond deeds as being alive in 1476. Nicholas Hacket was sovereign of Kilkenny in 1526 and again in 1534; he was still alive in 1537.

Ledwich 1781, 480; Shee 1813, 75-6; Graves and Prim 1857, 249-50:22; Langrishe 1879, 16:22; Carrigan 1905, iii, 155-6:22; Leslie 1933:11.

40. John Cantwell. 1531.
Rectangular slab with an eight-armed cross ending in fleur-de-lis terminals. Blackletter inscription:

> HIC IACET DNS JOHES CATWEL QUoDA P'SENTOR' ISTI ECCLIE Qi OBIIT XVIII DIE MES' NOVEBRIS Ao Di M CCCCC XXXI CUI' AIE P'PCIET' DS AME. MILO EPS OSS' OIB' DICETIB' OR'ONE DICA & SALVTACOE AG'LICA P' AIA P'DCI PNTORIS TOCIES QoCIES 'CESSIT XL DIES IDULGECIE.
> HIC IACET DNS JOHES NELE THESAURARI ISTI ECCLIE Qi OBIIT [   ].

> Translation: Here lies Master John Cantwell, formerly precentor of this church who died 18th November 1531. On whose soul may God have mercy. Amen. Milo, bishop of Ossory, has granted an indulgence of forty days each time to all who say an Our Father and Hail Mary for the soul of the said precentor.
> Here lies Master John Nele, treasurer of this church, who died [   ].

The Cantwell family has been settled in the Kilkenny area since the thirteenth century giving their name for instance to Cantwell's Court. On the other hand the Neles or Neils are rarely found. However a James Neales, burgess of Callan, was buried there in 1624.

Ledwich 1781, 480; Shee 1813, 72; Graves and Prim 1857, 180-82:20; Langrishe 1879, 15:20; Carrigan 1905, iii, 154-5:20.

41. Piers Butler and Margaret FitzGerald. 1539.
Double altar tomb. Effigies on mensa with carved side panels. The effigy of Piers Butler is shown in armour similar to that of James Schortals (no. 33) but the sword is suspended by a belt over the right shoulder. His head rests upon a pillow decorated on each side with an eagle displayed. His wife Margaret FitzGerald has her hands joined in prayer and wears a long gown of many pleats falling to the feet. The full sleeves are gathered in near the wrist with a band, beneath which are shown the laced sleeves of her kirtle. The V-neck is bordered by a narrow collar and rests low on the shoulders. The gown is tied at the waist by a buckled belt whose strap falls down the front of the gown and is embroidered with quatrefoils. On her head she wears a horned head-dress with reticulated sides from the back of which a veil, supported by two angels, falls to her shoulders. On the crown of the headress is a highly embroidered kerchief. Blackletter inscription:

> + INRI. HIC IACENT PETRUS BUTTELER COMES ORMONIE & OSS' Qi OBIIT XXVI DIE AUGUSTI Ao DNi M CCCCC XXXIX ET MARGARETA FI'GERALDE COMITISSA UXOR EI' Q OBIIT IX DIE AUGUSTI [   ].

Fig. 27. No. 41: Piers Butler and Margaret Fitzgerald. 1539.

Translation: Jesus of Nazareth, king of the Jews. Here lie Piers Butler earl of Ormond and Ossory who died 26th August 1539 and his wife Countess Margaret FitzGerald who died 9th August [   ].

The date of Piers Butler's birth is unclear but it is unlikely to have been before 1467. He married Margaret FitzGerald, daughter of Garret Mór, eight earl of Kildare in 1485. In 1505 he became the agent for the Irish lands of the absentee earl of Ormond and on the earl's death in 1515 Piers laid claim to the title on the grounds that he was the nearest legitimate male heir. In 1520 he became Lord Treasurer of Ireland and in 1522 he was appointed Lord Deputy. About 1527 Sir Thomas Boleyn, a descendant of the late earl in the female line, petitioned Henry VIII for the title of earl of Ormond. The king asked Piers Butler to surrender his title and on so doing Piers was created earl of Ossory in an elaborate ceremony at Windsor Castle in 1528. In 1538, after the death of Thomas Boleyn, the earldom of Ormond was restored to him. Margaret FitzGerald, noted by contemporaries for being strongminded and wise, died in 1542.

Fig. 28. No. 41: South side-panel showing the Arms of the Passion and Christ bound to the column.

The present monument was reassembled in the last century and its side panels are not the original ones. The head end shows the Crucifixion. The north side panel has six apostle in niches: SS Philip, Andrew, Simon, Thaddeus, James Major and Matthew; portion of this has been shown by Dr Rae to belong to the Schortal tomb (no. 33). The foot end has a Tudor rose on one side and the Butler coat of arms, identified by Graves and Prim as those of Thomas, the tenth earl of Ormond, on the other. The south panel shows the Crucifixion between the Virgin and St John flanked by the arms of Butler and Cantwell on one side, and Christ bound to a column, and the Arms of the Passion, on the other. The panels at the foot end may belong to the early seventeenth century but the others would appear to be of sixteenth century date. The south panel suggests that the cathedral possessed another double tomb, to a Butler and Cantwell, totally lost except for this portion.

Ledwich 1781, 467; Shee 1813, 47-9; Graves and Prim 1857, 182-249:21; Langrishe 1879, 15:21; Carrigan 1905, iii, 155:21; Phelan 1969, 64-66; Hunt 1974, 186-8: no. 142; Empey 1984.

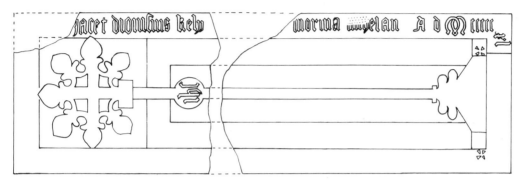

Fig. 29. No. 42. Denis Kely and Morina Whelan. 1540.

42. Denis Kely and Morina Whelan. 1540.
Rectangular slab with eight-armed segmental cross with fleur-de-lis terminals. In the centre of the cross-head is an IHS. Blackletter inscription in false relief:

> [HIC] IACET DIONISIUS KELY [E] .... MORINA [W]HELAN Ao Di M CCCCC XL

> Translation: Here lies Denis Kely [and his wife] Morina Whelan. A.D. 1540.

Ledwich 1781, 479; Graves and Prim 1857, 282-3:44; Langrishe 1879, 21:44; Carrigan 1905, iii, 164-5:44.

43. ? James Butler. c.1546?
Altar tomb. Effigy of knight on mensa. Sidepanels at the front and head end. The armour is identical to that of Piers Butler (no. 36) with the exception of the gauntlets, which differ. On either side of the head is the Butler shield: a chief indented. Uninscribed. The suggestion that this is the tomb of James Butler, ninth earl of Ormond, has gained general currency; if so, it may date to around 1546, the year of his death. More recently, Dr Stalley (1983) has suggested that the tomb may be a cenotaph, perhaps one of a number, erected by Piers Butler to commemorate his ancestors.

   The front panel shows six apostles: SS Peter, Matthew, Thomas, John, Paul and Bartholomew. The head end has a panel of tracery consisting of three quatrefoils. Both panels appear to be late insertions.

Graves and Prim 1857, 136; Langrishe 1879, 12:P136; Phelan 1969, 66-7; Hunt 1974, 188: no. 143.

Fig. 30. No. 43: ? James Butler. c.1546?   *Fig. 31. No. 44: Edmund Purcell and Ellen Grace. 1549.*

44.   Edmund Purcell and Ellen Grace. 1549.

Fragment of a rectangular slab, carved in false relief. The upper portion bears a cross surrounded by the instruments of the Passion. Below this is a miniature armoured effigy broken from the waist down. He wears overlapping plates on the body with a pisane protecting the neck and besagews on the shoulders. He wears a cap which appears to have been attached to the pisane. Marginal blackletter inscription:

[HIC IACET EDMUNDUS PURSELL] CAPITANEU' TURBARIOR[U]
COMITIS ORMONIE Qi OBIIT QUARTO DIE [N]OVEBRIS Ao DI M
CCCCC [XLIX] & ELLENA GRAS UX' EI' Ao DI M CCCCC [   ]

78

Translation: [Here lies Edmund Pursell] captain of the earl of Ormond's kerns who died 4th November 1549 and Ellen Grace his wife [who died] A.D. 15[   ].

The slab was broken before Graves' and Prim's time and the missing portion of the inscription is supplied from O'Phelan's transcript. Ledwich, however, gives the date as 1509.

Ledwich 1781, 466; Shee 1813, 67; Graves and Prim 1857, 250-2:23; Langrishe 1879, 16:23; Carrigan 1905, iii, 156-7:23; Hunt 1974, 188-89: no. 144.

45.   Edmund Purcell and Ellen Grace. 1549.
Rectangular slab with segmental cross ending in fleur-de-lis terminals and rising from a stepped base. Decorated with an IHS and a shield bearing the Purcell coat of arms. Marginal blackletter inscription:

> HIC IACET EDMUND' PURCELL CAPITANEU' TURBARIORU COMITIS ORMONIE Q. OBIIT QUARTO DIE [NOVEBRI]S [Ao Di M .... X] & ELLENA GRAS UX. EI' Q. OBIIT [   ] Ao Do M CCCCC [   ].

> Translation as for no. 44 which commemorates the same people. Nos. 44-5 Nos. 44-5 may have been part of a composite monument.

Langrishe 1879, 16:23a; Carrigan 1905, iii, 156:23a.

46.   Slab fragment. 1540x1550.
Fragment lying partially buried beside the north wall of the churchyard with blackletter inscription:

> .... OBIIT Ao Di M CCCCC XL ....

> Translation: .... who died A.D. 154 ....

Carrigan describes a slab in this location as belonging to a Dowli, merchant of Irishtown. The portion of the inscription visible at the moment, however, does not correspond to anything that Carrigan has transcribed.

Carrigan 1905, iii, 172 and 161.

47.   Uninscribed effigy. First half of 16th cent.
Altar tomb. Effigy of a lady on the mensa wearing a long gown dropping to her feet. She wears a mantle over the gown and holds the ends in her hands. Round her waist is a belt with a buckle. Over her throat and face is a veil which has a goffered upper edge across the forehead. Covering this is a second more voluminous veil falling onto her shoulders. The mode of dress suggests that the lady was a widow or vowess.

   The side panels do not appear to be original. The front panel is made up of two sections: on the left, a bishop and female saint; on the right, a female saint, St Catherine, St Mary Magdalen, and another unidentified female saint. The east end panel shows an archbishop while the west end has St Mary Magdalen.

Graves and Prim 1857, 137; Langrishe 1879, 12:E40; Hunt 1974, 190-1: no. 147.

Fig. 32. No. 47: Uninscribed effigy. First half of 16th cent.

Fig. 33. No. 47: Front panel.

48. Cottrell and Lawles. 1550 et seq.
Reused rectangular slab with floral decoration of late thirteenth century style. Now the top of an altar tomb. Very worn. Decorated with an IHS set within a circle and hands clasping a heart below. The rest of the surface is occupied with a blackletter inscription:

> HIC IACENT ADAM COTTRELL JACOB' COTTRELL RICARD' LAWLES ET WALTER LAWLES CU EI' UXORE LETICIA CoURCY QUODA BURGES' VILLE KILK[ENIE]' AC DNI DE TALBOTT IS INCHE Qi WALTER' OBIIT SCDO DIE MES' DECEBRIS Ao Di M CCCCC QiNQaGmo QUOR' AIAB P'PICIET' DE' AME.
> HIC IACET RICD' LAWLES FILIUS ET [   ] HERES DICTI WALTERI QUI OBIIT VI DIE MES' OCTOBRIS Ao DNI M CCCCC LIII.
> HIC IACET JACOB' LAWLES FRATER ET HERES RICDI LAWLES FILII ET HEREDIS WALTERI LAWLES [Qi] OBI[IT U]LTIo DIE JULII Ao DN M CCCCC LXII CUI' AIE P'PICIET' D[E'] AME [ET] ADAM LAWLES Qi OBIIT XX DIE OCTOBRIS 1600 [ET LETICIA] SHEE UXOR EI' Qe OBIIT [5] DIE OCTOBR' M CCCCC LXXVI.
> CREDO QD REDEPTOR ME' VIVIT & IN NOVISSIMO DIE DE TRA SURRECTUR' SU ET I CARNE MEA VIDEBO DEU SALVATORE MEU QUE VISUR' SU EGO IPSE & NON ALI' & OCULI MEI CONSPECTURI SUT.

Translation: Here lie Adam Cottrell, James Cottrell, Richard Lawles and Walter Lawles with his wife Leticia Courcy, formerly burgesses of the town of Kilkenny and lords of Talbott's Inch; which Walter died 2nd December 1550; on whose souls may God have mercy Amen.

Here lies Richard Lawles, the son and heir of the aforesaid Walter who died 6th October A.D. 1553.

Here lies James Lawles, brother and heir of Richard Lawles (the son and heir of Walter Lawles) who died on the last day of July 1562; on whose soul may God have mercy, Amen. And Adam Lawles who died 20th October 1600. [And Leticia] Shee his wife who died 5th October 1576.

I believe that my Redeemer lives, and on the last day I shall rise out of the earth, and in my flesh I shall see God, my Saviour, whom I shall see with my own eyes, I myself and no other.

Cotterell's (now Irishtown) bridge is mentioned as a placename in the early thirteenth century suggesting that members of that family were settled in Kilkenny at a very early stage of the Anglo-Norman invasion. Their principal property, however, appears to have been at Kells. The Lawlesses are present as merchants in the town of Kilkenny from the closing years of the fourteenth century. Of the individuals mentioned on this monument Walter Lawless was sovereign of Kilkenny in 1545 and Adam Lawless was portreeve of Irishtown in 1564.

The tomb front has an inserted panel of six ogee headed niches, which may have been part of a stone coffin or sarcophagus originally.

Ledwich 1781, 463; Shee 1813, 43; Graves and Prim 1857, 252-8:24; Langrishe 1879, 16:24; Carrigan 1905, iii, 157-8:24.

Fig. 34. No. 49: John Grace. 1552.

49. John Grace and Onorina Brenach. 1552.
Altar tomb. Damaged effigy on mensa of a knight in relief with side panels at the front, head and foot. The legs of the effigy are missing and the head is battered. The body defence consisted of a pair of plates with the habergeon projecting below. The neck and shoulders are protected by a pisane, pointed over the chest, and the arms are defended by sleeves of mail with mufflers extending over the hands. The legs were also defended by mail chausses with poleyns of plate at the knees. Portion of the bascinet remains and there is a belt at the waist. Blackletter inscription:

Fig. 35. No. 49: East end-panel: Grace arms.

82

HIC IACET JOHES GRAS MILES AC BARO DE COURTISTOWN &
ONORINA BRENACH UX EI' Ao DNi M CCCCC LII VIII DIE MES ....
RORICUS OTWNNE FABRICAVIT ISTAM TUBAM

Translation: Here lies John Grace, knight and baron of Courtstown, and
Onorina Brenach his wife .... 8th .... A.D. 1552
Rory O'Tunney made this tomb.

The Grace family appears to be associated with Courtstown from the thirteenth
century. John Grace and his wife Onorina rebuilt the chapel of Tullaroan in 1543
according to an inscription on the door there. This tomb would appear to have been
made in 1552 during Grace's lifetime as he is mentioned as a member of parliament for
County Kilkenny in 1568.

The front panel shows six apostles in niches: SS Peter, Andrew, John, James Major,
Thomas and James Minor. The head end is carved with a crucifixion flanked by the
Virgin and St John. The foot end had a shield with the Grace arms, a lion rampant. It is
not clear whether these panels belong to the tomb or not.

Harris 1764, i, fig. opp. p. 397; Ledwich 1781, 477; Shee 1813, 68; Shaw 1819, 567;
Grace 1823, 21; Graves and Prim 1857, 258-62:25; Langrishe 1879, 17:25; Carrigan
1905, iii, 158:25; Phelan 1969, 67-8; Hunt 1974, 189: no. 145.

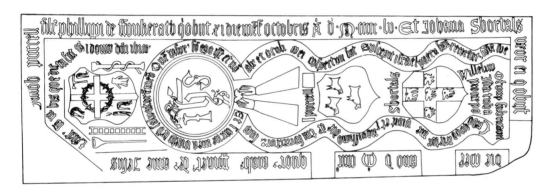

Fig. 36. No. 50: James Purcell and Johanna Shortals. 1552.

50. James Purcell and Johanna Shortals. 1552.
Rectangular slab similar to no. 48. Arms of the Passion at the head, and below it, an
IHS and two hands clasping a heart. Further down are the shields of Purcell and
Shortals. Blackletter inscription, like the decoration, in false relief:

[HIC IACEN]T JACOB' PURCELL FILI' PHILLIPPI DE FFOUKERATH Qi
OBIIT XI DIE MES' OCTOBRIS Ao Di M CCCCC LII. ET JOHANA
SHORTALS UXOR EI' Q OBIIT [   ] DIE MES' [   ] ANO Di M
CCCCC [   ] QUOR' AIAB' P'PICIET' DE' AME. JESUS. [MARIA].
CREDO QUOD REDETOR ME' VIVIT ET I NOVISSIMO DIE DE TRA
SURRECTUR' SUM ET I CARNE MEA VIDEBO DEU SALVATORE MEU
QUE VISUR' SU EGO IPE ET NO ALI' ET OCULI MEI COSPECTURI SUT.
SUSCEPIT ISRAEL PUERU SUU RECORDAT' MIE SUE. LETAT' SU IN
HIS QUE DICTA SUT Mi I DOMU DNI IBIM'.
WILLELIM' OTUNY FABRICAVIT ISTA TUBA PRO ME P'O'.

Translation: [Here lie] James Purcell, son of Phillip, of Foulksrath who died 11th October 1552. And his wife Johanna Schortals who died [   ] 15[   ]. On whose souls may God have mercy, Amen. Jesus. Mary.

I believe that my Redeemer lives, and on the last day I shall rise out of the earth, and in my flesh I shall see God, my Saviour, whom I shall see with my own eyes, I myself and no other. Remembering his mercy, He has received his servant Israel. I rejoiced in the things that were said to me, we shall go into the house of the Lord.

William O'Tunny made this tomb. Pray for me, I beseech you.

The Purcells were a prominent family in Co. Kilkenny during the fifteenth, sixteenth and seventeenth centuries and had their principal estates at Foulksrath and Ballyfoyle.

Ledwich 1781, 471; Shee 1813, 61-2; Graves and Prim 1857, 262-6:26; Langrishe 1879, 17:26; Carrigan 1905, iii, 158-9:26.

51. William Hay. 1557.
Rectangular slab. Decorated with the Arms of the Passion, a heart pierced by swords, and a chalice and host. Blackletter inscription in false relief, like the decoration:

+ HIC IACET RICARD' HAY' ET ANASTASIA KYGHO E.. UXOR Q....ICIET DE' AME. DNS. WILLMS HAY SBDECAN' ET VICARIUS DE DONFARTE OBIIT XVIII DIE JANUARII Ao DNi M CCCCC LVII. DA MICHI COR TU[U &]..FFESIT

Translation: Here lies Richard Hay and Anastasia Kygho (Keogh), his wife, [on whose souls] may God have mercy. Amen. Master William Hay, Dean's Vicar and vicar of Donfarte (Danesfort) died 18th January 1557.

Give me your heart and it is enough.

William Haye became vicar of Danesfort in 1551. The title of Dean's Vicar indicates that he was the head of the college of the vicars choral.

Graves and Prim 1857, 266:27; Langrishe 1879, 17:27; Carrigan 1905, iii, 159:27; Leslie 1933, 240.

52. Letitia Walme. 1560.
Fragmentary slab with segmental banded cross in false relief.
Blackletter inscription:

HIC I .... M CCCCC LXVI. ET LETICIA WALME UXOR EIUS Q OB[IIIT] [   ] DIE MES' [   ] ANO DNI M CCCCC LX [   ].

Translation: Here lie .... 1566. And Leticia Walme his wife who died [   ] day of the month of [   ] A.D. 1560

Ledwich 1781, 466; Graves and Prim 1857, 266:28; Langrishe 1879, 18:28; Carrigan 1905, iii, 159-60:28.

53. Nicholas Motyng. 1568.
Rectangular slab forming part of the seventeenth century mural tomb of the Murphys. Segmental cross, similar to no. 42, with IHS on stem. Marginal blackletter inscription in false relief:

HIC IACET HONEST' AC DIS .... S NICHOLAUS MOTYNG QUODA

CACELLARI' ISTI' ECC .... DE KILDER Qi OBIIT XIIII DIE MES' FEB'ARII
Ao Di M CCCCC LXVIII CUI' AIE P'PICIETUR DE' AME. JESUS+

Translation: Here lies the honest and discreet [man, Master] Nicholas Motyng,
formerly chancellor of this church [and rector] of Kilder [moyth] (now
Killermogh) who died 14th February 1568, on whose soul may God have
mercy. Amen. Jesus.

The Motyng family appear to have been based at Callan. Nicholas Motyng was
chancellor by 1530.

Ledwich 1781, 469; Shee 1813, 52; Graves and Prim 1857, 266-7:29; Langrishe 1879,
18:29; Carrigan 1905, iii, 160:29; Leslie 1933, 84.

Fig. 37. No. 54: Cross slab fragment. 1570.

54. Cross slab. 1570.
Slab fragment, rectangular, ornamented with an eight-armed interlaced cross in false
relief parts of which are very worn. Blackletter inscription:

.... M CCCCC LXX Q ....

Translation: .... 1570 ....

Langrishe 1879, 18:29a; Carrigan 1905, iii, 160:29a.

85

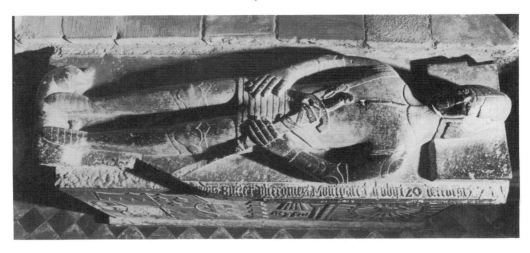

Fig. 38. No. 55: Richard Butler. 1571.

Fig. 39. No. 55: Front panel.

55. Richard Butler. 1571.
Altar tomb. Effigy of knight in relief on mensa. The figure has a breast plate with lames below; the legs and arms are protected by plates. Pointed bascinet with gorget protecting the neck. Gauntlets on the hands and sabatons of mail on the feet. The

86

sword is hung from a belt worn across the shoulder. Blackletter inscription in false relief:

> HIC IAC[ET NOBls Ds RICHA]RDUS BUTLER VICECOMES MONTGARET Qi OBIIT 20 DECEBRS 1571

> Translation: Here lies the most noble Lord Richard Butler, Viscount Mountgarret, who died 20th December 1571.

Richard Butler was the second son of Piers, earl of Ormond, and Margaret FitzGerald (no. 41, above). He was created a viscount in 1550. The tomb front is original and is carved in low relief with the Butler shield quartered and differenced by a crescent showing that Richard was the second son. The letters R and B flank the shield and on the right are the instruments of the Passion.

Harris 1764, i, fig. opp. p. 397; Ledwich 1781, 473; Shee 1813, 64; Graves and Prim 1857, 268-70:31; Langrishe 1879, 18:31; Carrigan 1905, iii, 160:31; Hunt 1974, 189-90: no. 146.

56. Joanna Nowlan. 1575.

Plain rectangular slab broken into two pieces with worn marginal blackletter inscription:

> H[IC IACET . . . . QNDA BU]RGE[S KILKENNIE Qi OBIIT . . . . DIE ME]NSIS FEBRUAR[II 15]8[1]. ET JOANNA [NO]WLAN [UXOR EI' Q] O[BIIT V] DIE MENSIS DECEMBRIS [1575].

> Translation: Here lies . . . . sometime burgess of Kilkenny who died 5th February 1581. And Joanna Nowlan his wife who died 5th December 1575.

Graves and Prim read the initial inscription as commemorating Patrick Kerin but to Carrigan it was Peter Mylotte; it is now obliterated.

Ledwich 1781, 464; Shee 1813, 43; Graves and Prim 1857, 270:32; Langrishe 1879, 18:32; Carrigan 1905, iii, 160:32.

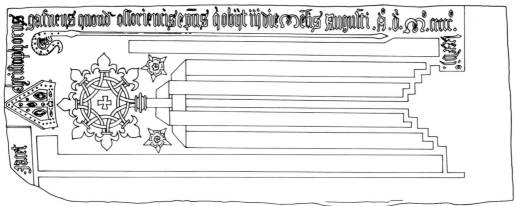

Fig. 40. No. 57: Christopher Gafney. 1576.

57. Christopher Gafney. 1576.

Rectangular slab ornamented with a banded interlaced cross with a small cross in the centre of the cross-head. In original position. Episcopal mitre and staff carved in false relief. Blackletter inscription:

[HIC] IACET CHRISTOPHORUS GAFNEUS QUOND' OSSORIENSIS
EPUS Qi OBIIT III DIE M[ES]IS AUGUSTI Ao Di M CCCCC LXXVI.

Translation: Here lies Christopher Gafney, formerly bishop of Ossory, who died 3rd August 1576.

Christopher Gafney became bishop of Ossory in 1567.

Ware 1665, 149; Harris 1764, i, fig. opp. p. 397; Shee 1813, 80; Graves and Prim 1857, 270-1; Langrishe 1879, 19:33; Carrigan 1905, iii, 161:33.

58. Nicholas Walshe. 1585.
Plain altar tomb. Undisturbed, still retaining its mortar sealing and traces of whitewash. Blackletter inscription:

HIC IACET REVEREND' PATER NICOLAUS WALSHE QoND' OSSOR'
EPUS Qi OBIIT DIE MES' DECEBRIS XIIII Ao Di M Vc LXXXV.

Translation: Here lies the Reverend Father Nicholas Walshe, formerly Bishop of Ossory, who died 14th December, 1585.

Nicholas Walsh succeeded Christopher Gaffney as bishop of Ossory in 1577. He was a native of Waterford and had studied at Oxford, Cambridge and Paris. At the time of his appointment he was chancellor of St Patrick's Cathedral, Dublin. He commenced a translation of the New Testament into Irish and participated in the printing of the first work in Irish type, a catechism, while at Dublin in 1571. He was murdered in 1585 by James Dullard against whom he was proceeding for adultery at the time.

Ware 1665, 149; Harris 1764, i, 419 and fig. opp. p. 397; Ledwich 1781, 478; Shee 1813, 69-70; Graves and Prim 1857, 271-2:35; Langrishe 1879, 19:35; Carrigan 1905, iii, 161:35; Leslie 1933, 14-5; Quin 1984.

59. Charles and Frederick-Phillip Bourcier. 1584 and 1587. Mural plaque with heraldic shield and blackletter inscription in relief:

QUI CLARI FUERANT FILI SPESQ' ALMA PARENTU
BOURCHERI CHAROLUS FREDERICUSQ' PHILIPPUS
OSSA IMMATURA SIMUL FLEBILIS NUNC CONTIGIT URNA
MORTE PUER JUVENIS VIRQ. SENEXQ' CADIT
QUORUM ALTER OBIIT [17 DIE SE]PTEMBRIS [1584]
ALTER VIII DIE MARTII Ao 1587.

Translation: Charles and Frederick-Philip Bourcier who were the fair sons and fond hope of their parents. The mournful urn now covers their immature remains together. By death falls the boy, the youth, the man in his prime, the aged. One of them died on the 17th September 1584, the other on the 8th March 1587.

The shield is exceptional for the number of armorial bearings shown on it. The dexter side is a quarterly of ten showing the arms of: Bourcier, Louvain, FitzWarine, Audley, Cogan, Hankford, Stapleton, Martin, Dynham, and Arches. The arms on the sinister side are those of the duke of Norfolk: Howard, Plantagenet, Warren, Mowbray. The knots below the shield are known as 'Bourcier knots'.

Sir George Bourcier was a son of the second earl of Bath and came to Ireland as a military captain in 1567 and spent the early part of his career in Munster being knighted in 1579. He died in 1605.

Ledwich 1781, 465; Shee 1813, 45; Graves and Prim 1857, 272-3:36; Langrishe 1879, 19:36; Langrishe 1904-5; Carrigan 1905, iii, 161-2:36.

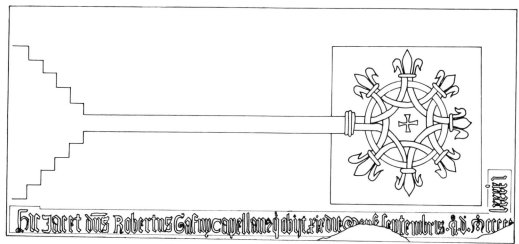

Fig. 41. No. 60. Robert Gafney. 1591.

60. Robert Gaffney. 1591.
Rectangular slab decorated with a banded eight-armed interlaced cross rising from a stepped base, in false relief. Blackletter inscription:

> HIC IACET DNS ROBERTUS GAFNY CAPELLAN' Qi OBIIT XIX DIE MENS' SEPTEMBRIS Ao Di M CCCCC LXXXXI

> Translation: Here lies Master Robert Gafny, chaplain, who died 19th September A.D. 1591.

Robert Gaffney was appointed treasurer of Ossory in 1563 and precentor in 1576. In his will he gave 10s. towards the repair of the 'parish chapel of St Canice's'.

Shee 1813, 80; Graves and Prim 1857, 273:37; Langrishe 1879, 19:37; Carrigan 1905, iii, 162:37; Leslie 1933, 74-5.

61. David Pembrock et al. 1590 et seq.
Slab fragment ornamented with a banded segmental cross. Marginal blackletter inscription continued on bands:

> [H]IC IACET TH[OMAS PEMBROCK QUONDA B]URGES' VILLE KILKENIE QUI OBII[T X] DIE SEPTEBR' Ao DNi .... [ET DAVID PEM]B[ROCK] FILIUS DCTI THOME Qi OBIIT 14 DIE MESIS OC[TOBRIS Ao Di] 1590. [ET THOM]AS FILIUS DICTI DAVID UNA CUM [EIUS UXORIBUS ALICI]A RAGGET & KATHARINA ARCHER. [DICTUS TH]OMAS OBIIT 25 JANUARII 1616 [ET FUIT] UNUS PRIMORUM VICECOMITUM [KILKENIE. DICTA ALICIA RAGGET] OBIIT 21 [DIE MESIS .... 15]85. KATHARINA ARCHER OBIIT .... US FILIUS DICTI THOME PEMBROCK .... JOANNA RAGGET UXOR DICTI ....

Translation: Here lies Thomas Pembrock, formerly a burgess of the town of Kilkenny, who died on the 10th September A.D. .... And David Pembrock, son of the said Thomas, who died 14th October 1590. And Thomas, son of the said David, with his wives Alicia Ragget and Katharina Archer. The said Thomas died 25th January 1616 and was one of the first sheriffs of Kilkenny [city]. The said Alicia Ragget died 21 .... 1585. Katharina Archer died .... son of the said Thomas Pembrock .... Joanna Ragget wife of the said ....

The Pembrokes were settled in Kilkenny from the beginning of the fourteenth century. The David Pembroke of the monument was portreeve of Irishtown in 1575, and in 1594 his son Thomas filled this office. When the corporation of Kilkenny received a new charter in 1609 designating the town a city and its chief magistrate a mayor, Thomas Pembroke and Walter Ryan were nominated its first two sheriffs. This is the circumstance alluded to on the monument.

Ledwich 1781, 467-8; Shee 1813, 49; Graves and Prim 1857, 274-5:38; Langrishe 1879, 19:38; Carrigan 1905, iii, 162:38.

Fig. 42. No. 62: Honorina Grace. 1596.

62.   Honorina Grace. 1596.
Altar tomb. Effigy of a recumbent woman with her hands joined in prayer on the mensa; decorated front panel (not original). She wears a long gown falling in folds to her feet; the sleeves are full and are gathered below the wrist with a band, beneath which the plain sleeves of her kirtle can be seen. She has five rings on her fingers and another on the thumb of her left hand. The V-neck of the gown has a broad collar matching the band on the sleeves. She has a horned head-dress with reticulated sides and a kerchief between the points. A veil falls from the head-dress on to her shoulders. The gown is buckled at the waist by a highly decorated belt whose strap hangs down the front of the gown. The face is very crudely executed. Marginal blackletter inscription:

HIC IACET HONORINA GRAS FILIA JOHIS GRACE MILITIS AC QUOND' UXOR OLIVERI SHORTALL DNI DE BALLILORCAN Q OBIIT 6 DIE MESiS DECEMBER Ao Di M CCCCC 96.

Translation: Here lies Honorina Grace daughter of John Grace, knight, and formerly wife of Oliver Shortall, lord of Ballylarkin, who died 6 December 1596.

Fig. 43. No. 62: Front panel.

The style of dress on this monument is very similar to that of Margaret FitzGerald (no. 41) dated 1539 and Hunt comments that this tomb may have been made some time before 1596.

The front panel shows six apostles in pointed niches: SS Philip, Bartholomew, Matthew, Simon, Thaddeus, and Mathias.

Langrishe 1879, 20:38a; Carrigan 1905, iii, 162–3:38a; Phelan 1969, 68–9:5; Hunt 1974, 191–2: no. 148.

Fig. 44. No. 63: William Donoghou. 1597.

63. William Donoghou. 1597.
Rectangular slab decorated by a four armed cross with fleur-de-lis terminals; the cross head has a combination of rectilinear and curvilinear interlace, and the shaft rises from a calvary. On either side of the cross are the instruments of the Passion with the sun

and moon above. Marginal blackletter inscription in false relief:

> HIC IACET GUILIELM' DONOGHOU QUONDA BURGENSIS VILLE DE IRISTOUNE IUXTA KILKENIA Qi OBIIT XIII DIE MES' NOBEMBRIS Ao Di 1597 & CATHERINA MONI EI' UXOR Qae OBIIT [   ]

> Translation: Here lies William Donoghou, formerly burgess of Irishtown, by Kilkenny, who died 13th November A.D. 1597 and Catherine Moni, his wife, who died [   ]

The Ui Donnchadha (anglised both as O'Donoghue and Dunphy) were an important family in north Kilkenny from before the twelfth century. The William Donoghue commemorated here was portreeve of Irishtown in 1582.

Ledwich 1781, 469; Shee 1813, 53; Graves and Prim 1857, 275-6:39; Langrishe 1879, 20:39; Carrigan 1905, iii, 163:39.

64. Ellena Butler. 1597.
Rectangular slab ornamented with a cross similar to no. 63, flanked by the instruments of the Passion. Marginal blackletter inscription in false relief:

> [HIC] IACENT ILL'S Da ELLENA BUTLER NOBILISSI VIRI Di PETRI BUTLER ORMONIAE COMITIS FILIA & UX[OR QUOND]A PIA CLARISSIMI Di DONALDI OBRIEN TUMUNDIAE COMITIS Q OBIIT 2 JULII 1597

> Translation: Here lie the illustrious Lady Ellena Butler, daughter of the most noble Lord Piers Butler, earl of Ormond, and pious wife of the most illustrious Lord Donald O'Brien, earl of Thomond, who died 2 July 1587.

Ellen Butler was the sixth and youngest daughter of Piers Butler and was married to Donald O'Brien before 1533. Her husband died in 1553 and she appears to have survived him by forty-four years.

Ledwich 1781, 469; Shee 1813, 52; Graves and Prim 1857, 277-8:40; Langrishe 1879, 20:40; Carrigan 1905, iii, 163:40.

65. James Sentleger. 1597.
Rectangular slab, plain except for a worn escutcheon charged with a bend, and above it, according to Graves and Prim, the words BIN GULEN ARGEN. Marginal blackletter inscription in false relief:

> HIC IACENT JACOBUS SENTLEGER DE BALLEFENNON [QUI OBIIT PRI]MO DIE FEB[RUARII 1597 ET E]GIDIA TOBEN [EI' UXOR Q OBIIT 2] DIE MENSIS NOVEMBRIS 1570 ET PATRICIUS SENTLEGER FILIUS SECUNDUS EOR' Qi OBIIT XXI DIE MENSIS FEBRUARII 1607, ET MARGARETA [SHEE EI'] UXOR Q OBIIT [   ] DIE MENSIS [   ]

> Translation: Here lie James St Leger of Ballyfennon, who died 1st February 1597 and Egidia Toben, his wife, who died 2nd November 1570. And Patrick St Leger their second son who died 21st February 1607. And Margaret Shee his wife who died [   ] day of the month of [   ]

The St Leger family was based at Tullaghanbrogue since the thirteenth century. The Ballyfennon St Legers appear to have been a branch of these.

Ledwich 1781, 464; Shee 1813, 44; Graves and Prim 1857, 279-80; Langrishe 1879, 20:41; Carrigan 1905, iii, 163-4:41.

66.   George Savadge. 16th cent.
Rectangular slab with interlaced segmental cross similar to no. 60. Marginal blackletter inscription in false relief, now very worn:

> HIC IACET GEORGIUS SAVADGE FILIUS GEORGII SAVADGE QUONDAM VILLE KILKENNIE BURGENSIS Qi OBIIT [   ] DIE MENSIS [   ] AN. D M CCCCC [   ].

> Translation: Here lies George Savadge son of George Savadge, formerly burgess of the town of Kilkenny, who died the [   ] day of the month of [   ] A.D. 15[   ].

Subsequently the following inscription was added in Roman capitals:

> HIC IACET .... FILIVS MARGARETA SAWADGE.

> Here lies .... son of Margaret Sawadge.

The Savages were an important merchant family in Kilkenny from the fifteenth century. According to Carrigan they also wrote their name as Seix (pronounced Size).

Ledwich 1781, 477; Shee 1813, 68; Graves and Prim 1857, 281:42; Langrishe 1879, 20:42; Carrigan 1905, iii, 164:42.

67.   Thomas Sawage and Nichola Shee. 16th cent.
Fragment of a rectangular slab ornamented with a cross similar to no. 57. Marginal blackletter inscription in false relief:

> HIC IACET THOMAS SAWAGE QUODA BURGENSIS .... [N]ICOLAA SCHEE UXOR EI' Q OBIIT [   ] DIE MES' [   ] Ao Di M CCCCC
> [   ]

> Translation: Here lies Thomas Sawage formerly burgess .... Nicolaa Shee, his wife, who died the [   ] day of the month of [   ] A.D. 15[   ].

A later inscription in Roman capitals runs along the shaft of the cross:

> .... HARDVS CANTWELL

> Richard Cantwell

Graves and Prim suggest that Thomas Sawage may have been merchant of that name from Irishtown referred to in 1537. It is impossible to be certain, however.

Ledwich 1781, 479; Shee 1813, 68; Graves and Prim 1857, 282:43; Langrishe 1879, 21:43; Carrign 1905, iii, 164:43.

68.   Ellen ? 16th cent.
Rectangular slab with banded eight-armed cross in false relief. Marginal blackletter inscription:

> HIC IACET ELENA ....

> Translation: Here lies Ellen ....

Langrishe 1879, 21:43a; Carrigan 1905, iii, 164:43a.

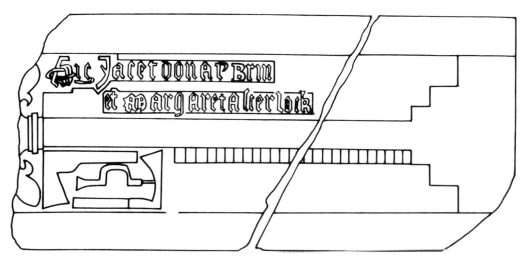

Fig. 45. No. 69. Donatus Brin and Margaret Scerlock. 16th cent.

69. Donatus Brin and Margaret Scerlock. 16th cent.
Lower part of a rectangular slab decorated with a cross shaft rising from a stepped base. Two adzes, an auger and a carpenter's square are carved in relief on one side of the cross, with a blackletter inscription on the other:

HIC IACET DONAT' BRIN ET MARGARETA SCERLOCK

Translation: Here lies Donatus Brin (Byrne) and Margaret Scerlock (Sherlock).

Ledwich 1781, 480; Shee 1813, 75; Graves and Prim 1857, 283:45; Langrishe 1879, 21:45; Carrigan 1905, iii, 165:45.

Fig. 46. No. 70: Belina Shee. 16th cent.

70. Belina Shee. 16th cent.
Slab fragment with portion of the base of a cross similar to that of John Moghlande (no. 34). Blackletter inscription in false relief:

.... & BELINA SHEE UX[OR] DCTI THOME .... OBIIT [   ] RICHARD OBIIT ....

Translation: .... and Belina Shee, wife of the said Thomas .... died [   ] Richard died ....

Graves and Prim 1857, 283:46; Langrishe 1879, 21:46; Carrigan 1905, iii, 165:46.

94

71. M.B. 16th cent.
Rectangular slab decorated with an eight-armed cross in false relief and the letters M. B. in Roman capitals.

Langrishe 1879, 21:44a.

Fig. 47. No. 72: Fragment of a knight's leg.

72. Effigial fragment. 16th cent.
Resting against the wall of the north aisle on no. 79 is the knee portion of a knight's leg, protected by plates. The greaves are present with one hinge. The poleyn has a scalloped border with secondary plates extending up and down the leg.

Hunt 1974, 189; Bradley 1980, 16: no. 61.

73. Fragments of a tomb chest. 16th cent.
Underneath the thirteenth century canopied niche in the north transept are two end panels set together to form one long panel. The dexter panel shows three figures under pointed niches: St James Minor, an unidentified saint, and St Andrew. The sinister slab shows Christ displaying his wounds, an archbishop, and a king.

Phelan 1969, 69-70:6; Hunt 1974, 192: no. 149.

74. Fragment of a tomb front. 16th cent.
It consists of five figures in niches separated by twisted columns and part of a sixth figure. The figures are SS Bartholomew, Simon, Matthew, Thaddeus, and Matthias. The sixth figure cannot be identified. The slab is a companion of no. 75 and Dr Rae has shown that these formed part of the tomb-chest of James Schortals (no. 33).

Rae 1966; Phelan 1969, 70:7; Hunt 1974, 192: no. 150.

Fig. 48. No. 73: 16th cent. tomb chest fragments reset underneath the thirteenth century canopied niche in the north transept.

Fig. 49. No. 74: Tomb front fragment. 16th cent.

75. Fragments of a tomb front. 16th cent.
Leaning against the west wall of the north aisle are two fragments forming the sinister end of a long tomb front. They are similar in style to no. 74 and come from the same monument. Four saints are represented in pointed niches: SS John, Thomas, James Minor and Philip.

Rae 1966; Phelan 1969, 70:8; Hunt 1974, 192: no. 151.

Fig. 50. No. 75: Tomb front fragment. 16th cent.

Fig. 51. No. 76: End panel of a tomb chest. Late 16th cent.?

76. End panel of a tomb chest. Late 16th cent.(?)
Beside no. 74 is a slab with a figure of the Trinity. God the Father holds the cross in his arms and the Holy Spirit is shown above his right shoulder.

Hunt 1974, 193: no. 152; Roe 1979, 137: no. 15

77. Tomb front fragment. 16th cent.
Against the west wall of the north aisle beside no. 75 is a fragment showing two figures. The dexter figure carries a book and would appear to be St John; the other is Christ displaying His wounds.

Phelan, 1969, 70; Hunt 1974, 193: no. 153.

Fig. 52. No. 78: Female saint with the Butler shield above.

Fig. 53. No. 78: St Gabriel.

Fig. 54. No. 78: Female saint, perhaps St Catherine.

78. Fragments in the east gable of the sexton's house. 16th cent.

Four figures have been built into the wall. The uppermost is a female saint with the Butler shield in the right spandrel. The figure on the lower left is an abbess with a crozier. The next figure is St Gabriel, holding a scroll in his right hand; he presumably comes from what was originally an Annunciation scene. The lowest figure appears to be a female saint and Hunt suggests that she may be St Catherine.

Hunt 1974, 193: no. 154.

Fig. 55. No. 79: End panel of a tomb chest. 16th cent.

79.   End panel of a tomb chest. 16th cent.
Lying against the north wall of the north aisle beside no. 49 is a rectangular panel decorated with foliage ornament.

80.   Side panel of an altar tomb. ? Late 16th cent.
Immediately west of the door in the north aisle is about two-thirds of a damaged panel displaying the instruments of the Passion.

81.   Uninscribed slab. 16th cent.
Rectangular slab with an eight-armed banded cross rising from a stepped base, carved in false relief. It may belong to the second half of the sixteenth century and may be dated on the basis of its similarity to no. 57.

Langrishe 1879, 12:C.

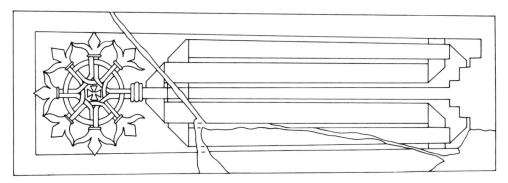

Fig. 56. No. 81: Uninscribed slab. 16th cent.

100

MISSING TOMBS

82. Hugh de Mapilton. 1260.
Ware (1665, 142) describes seeing this tomb near St Mary's chapel and records it as an effigy of exquisite workmanship (*statua operis exquisiti ornatum*).

83. Geoffrey St Leger. 1286.
Ware (1665, 142) describes this as a carved effigy (*statua . . . affabre ornato*) and says that it was situated beside that of Bishop de Mapilton.

84. Thomas Barry. 1459.
According to Ware (1665, 146) he was buried in front of the high altar.

85. David Hacket. 1479.
Ware (1665, 147) says that he was buried near the high altar.

86. John O'Hedian. 1486.
According to Ware (1655, 147) he was buried in a chapel beside the west door.

87. Oliver Cantwell. 1526.
Ware (1665, 147) states that he was buried in the Dominican Friary nearby, but that another monument was erected to his memory in St Canice's showing him in the habit of a Dominican.

88. William Vale. 1571.
Graves and Prim describe this as a fragmentary floor slab very much defaced and injured. It had a blackletter inscription:

> [HIC IA]CET DNS WILL' VALE QUODA . . . . IU' ECCLIE Qi OBIIT XXI DIE MES' . . . . M VC LXXI

> Translation: Here lies Master William Vale formerly . . . . of this church, who died the 21st day of the month of . . . . 1571.

Langrishe confuses this slab with no. 29, also commemorating a William Vayl, and notes it as mising in 1879.

Ledwich 1781, 471; Shee 1813, 61; Graves and Prim 1857, 267-8:30; Langrishe 1879, 18:30; Carrigan 1905, iii, 160.

89. Dowli. 1579.
Graves and Prim describe this as a fragment of a floor slab with an interlaced cross similar to no. 61. A portion of it was still surviving in the churchyard when Carrigan saw it but even that is now missing. It had a blackletter inscription:

> . . . . [D]OWLI QUOND' MARCATOR [ET] BURGES' VILLE HIBERNICANE KILKENI Qi OBIIT 8 DIE [   ] . . . . E BURGESIS Qi OBIIT [   ] DIE MENSIS [   ] ET ELINA . . . . UXOR EI'.Q. OBIIT 30 DIE MENSIS MARCII 1579.

Translation: .... [D]owli, formerly burgess and merchant of the Irishtown of Kilkenny, who died on the 8th day of [   ] .... burgess, who died the .... day of the month of [   ], and Elina .... his wife, who died on the 30th day of the month of March, 1579.

Ledwich 1781, 476; Graves and Prim 1857, 271:34; Langrishe 1879, 19:34; Carrigan 1905, iii, 161:34.

REFERENCES

Bradley, J. 1980.
'Some new and neglected medieval tomb slabs and fragments from Kilkenny', *Old Kilkenny Review,* New Ser. 2, No. 2, 5-21.

Bradley, J. In press.
'Medieval sarcophagi from Ireland', in MacNiocaill, G., and Wallace, P. F. (eds.) *Keimelia: studies in archaeology and history: essays in memory of Tom Delaney,* forthcoming.

Carrigan, W. 1905.
The history and antiquities of the diocese of Ossory. 4 vols. Dublin.

Egan, P. M. 1884.
The illustrated guide to the city and county of Kilkenny. Kilkenny.

Egan, P. M. 1895
'The Keteller monument, Kilkenny', *Jrl. Roy. Soc. Antiqs. Ireland* 25 (1895), 72-78.

Empey, C. A. 1984.
'From rags to riches: Piers Butler, earl of Ormond 1515-39', *Jrl. Butler Soc.* vol. 2, no. 2, 299-314.

Grace, S. 1823.
Memoirs of the family of Grace, London.

Graves, J. and Prim, J. G. A. 1857.
The history, architecture and antiquities of the cathedral church of St Canice, Kilkenny. Dublin.

Harris, W. 1764.
The whole works of Sir James Ware concerning Ireland, 2 vols. Dublin.

Hogan, J. 1874-9.
'Notes on an uninscribed monument in St Canice's Cathedral, Kilkenny', *Trans. Ossory Archaeol. Soc.* 1, 73-78.

Hunt, J. 1950.
'Rory O'Tunney and the Ossory tomb sculptures', *Jrl. Roy. Soc. Antiqs. Ireland* 80, 22-8.

Hunt, J. 1974.
Irish medieval figure sculpture 1200-1600. 2 vols. Dublin-London.

Langrishe, R. 1879.
Handbook to the Cathedral Church of St Canice, Kilkenny. Kilkenny.

Langrishe R. 1904-5.
'The Bourcier tablet in the cathedral church of St Canice, Kilkenny, with some account of that family', *Jrl. Royal Soc. Antiqs. Ireland* 34 (1904), 365-79; 35 (1905), 21-33.

Ledwich, E. 1781.
The history and antiquities of Irishtown and Kilkenny from original records and authentic documents. No. 9 of C. Vallencey (ed.) *Collectanea de Rebus Hibernicis.* Dublin.

Leslie, J. B. 1933.
Ossory clergy and parishes. Enniskillen.

Neary, A. 1984.
'Richard Ledrede: English Franciscan and bishop of Ossory', *Jrl. Butler Soc.* vol. 2, no. 3, 273-82.

Phelan, M. M. 1969.
'An amateur looks at the Ossory tombs with apostolic surrounds', *Old Kilkenny Review* No. 21, 60-75.

Quin, C. W. C. 1984.
'Nicholas Walsh and his friends: a forgotten chapter in the Irish Reformation', *Jrl. Butler Soc.* vol. 2, no. 3, 294-8.

Rae, E. C. 1966.
'An O'Tunney masterpiece reconstituted', *Old Kilkenny Review* No. 18, 62-71.

Roe, H. M. 1979.
'Illustrations of the Holy Trinity in Ireland: 13th to 17th centuries', *Jrl. Royal Soc. Antiqs. Ireland* 109, 101-150.

Shaw, R. 1819.
'Parish of Tullaroan, county of Kilkenny and diocese of Ossory', in Mason, W. S., *A statistical account or parochial survey of Ireland*, vol. 3. Dublin. 498-652.

Shee, P. 1813
(ed.) *Epigrafai monumentorum Basilicae Ossoriensi Sancto Canico sacrae: epitaphs on the tombs in the cathedral church of St Canice, Kilkenny, collected by John O'Phelan*. Dublin.

Stalley, R. 1983.
'Irish medieval tomb sculpture: some curiosities and queries', *Bulletin of the International Society for the Study of Church Monuments* 8 (1983), 172.

Ware, J. 1665.
De Praesulibus Hiberniae. Dublin.

ACKNOWLEDGEMENTS

The recording of these monuments has been spread over a number of years and I especially wish to thank Mr Edward Bourke, B.A. for the many hours of blood, sweat and tears which he put into describing and drawing these monuments during the autumns of 1980 and 1981. In the course of our long visitations we have always received the greatest assistance and help from Mr George Wilde and it is a particular pleasure to have the opportunity of thanking him here. I am grateful to Mr Niall Brady, B.A., for his help with the line drawings, to Mrs. H. A. King for figs. 47 and 55, and to Pieterse-Davison International for all of the other photographs.